Praise for It's All about Leadership— Be a Leader Worth Following

"How did King David – a man after God's heart – lovingly and effectively lead God's people? Drawing on Psalm 78:72 Dr. Jimmy Knott with simplicity, preciseness, and Holy Spirit insight reveals how to be a Leader Worth Following. His new book adapted from his video teachings and small group discussions looks at the importance of Authentic Character, Exceptional Competency, and Relational Connection in a Leader Worth Following. During this study you examine yourself as perhaps your toughest leadership challenge. Are leaders born or can they be developed? Interesting question. See what Jimmy and the Bible have to say about this and how we ALL can learn to be better Servant Leaders. And thus a Leader Worth Following! If you do you will be honoring God and having greater Godly influence and impact!"

– Tommy Beck
Vice President-Legacy Strategies, Compass

"I don't know of anyone who has more insight into leadership than Jimmy Knott. His work emerges from thirty-five years of being field tested, personally experienced, and put into practice. No theory. Real life. Good in the secular or church world. If I'm training leaders, after the Bible, this is my primary source."

– Dr. Jim Henry
Pastor Emeritus, First Baptist Orlando

"Being a student of leadership for over 40 years, I have read many books, and find Pastor Jimmy Knott's book titled *"It's All About Leadership – Be a Leader Worth Following,"* to be one of the very best teachings available on leadership. Based on a strong biblical foundation, it offers material that is not only comprehensive, but tangible and practical as well. Imparting wisdom that is real, the lessons learned can be applied to many aspects of one's life. This book has been extremely helpful to me and I believe that anyone who reads it will benefit greatly. It is a valuable tool that has provided insight in my continuing journey to become a better leader, and one that is worth following."

– **Duane Kuck**
President of Regal Marine Industries, Inc.

"For more than 6 years, my Executive MBA (EMBA) and Professional Master of Science in Management (PMSM) students and I have been privileged to have Dr. Jimmy Knott share a little of his leadership knowledge, experience, and wisdom each time I have taught Executive Leadership. He is engaging, challenges their concepts of leadership, and provides these graduate students with practical and immediately helpful leadership principles. Student feedback has always been extremely positive with many comments that what Dr. Knott shared with them was not only helpful but often life-impacting. The wisdom contained in this book reflects decades of study, insights, and application that will significantly benefit each reader."

– **Greg Mathison, M.S., Ph.D.**

"Pastor Jimmy Knott is an outstanding example of a strong Christian leader. He demonstrates a unique understanding of leadership and he is exceptional at communicating a clear and compelling vision for what godly men should aspire to. Jimmy delivers his powerful message in a simple, concise manner that has enriched the lives of many men, and made a positive impact on their families. He provides many clear biblical examples regarding leadership that point to the path of being a leader worthy of being followed. The net of this leadership journey is that we elevate our skills by focusing on connection, competency, and character. Jimmy is a leader that is worthy of being followed. This book shows us how to be that strong leader as well by being a stronger Christian!"

– **Dave Pickens**
Retired Darden Executive

"Jimmy Knott is one of the most gifted Bible teachers I have ever known. He is blessed with an uncanny ability to unpack scriptural truth and apply biblical principles to everyday life. I am pleased he has set his focus on leadership with this book. Jimmy is a shining example of a leader who has been forged through fire. Jimmy's teaching is always highly informational in style. His content, style, and delivery is usually very "textbook" in nature. His insights are very real and his applications are right on target. I recommend *It's All about Leadership* to anyone who desires to lead a life of purpose that positively impacts others along the way."

– **Kris DenBesten**
CEO Vermeer Southeast

"Jimmy Knott has a passion to develop leaders and his gift of teaching is sprinkled throughout this book as he offers valuable leadership principles that are both practical and relevant. I have served as a coach under Jimmy's leadership for many years and have had the privilege of witnessing lives that have been impacted as men realized and elevated their influence as a leader in the marketplace, the church, and at home. Read on and discover the nuggets of wisdom that await as you, too, unleash your potential as a leader worth following."

– **Paul V. Kraus**
Principal, Ronald Blue & Co.

IT'S
ALL ABOUT
LEADERSHIP

Be a Leader Worth Following

Dr. Jimmy Knott

ISBN 9781498478335

www.xulonpress.com

Dedication

To Linda, my high school sweetheart and bride of forty-plus years, who has always been there to encourage me to be all I could be for God.

Acknowledgements

Growing as a leader and writing a book about leadership is never a solo effort. I want to say thanks to:

- Jim Henry and David Uth for believing in me as a leader.

- The awesome faith community at First Baptist Orlando for over thirty-five years for being gracious and patient as I grew as a leader.

- All those, mostly in my church, who took the leadership plunge as I developed this material over many years.

- The DenBestens, Kucks, Mathisons, and Peacocks for believing in me and serving as my book launch team.

- Karen Naquin for transcribing the leadership live sessions.

- Donna George for being the best executive assistant on the planet!

- My precious Savior and Lord for calling me to lead in His service.

Table of Contents

FOREWORD

"It's all about leadership" seems so cliché but at the same time seems so right. There is no better way to describe the life and ministry of Jimmy Knott. This is what he bleeds every day. As I've heard him say many times, "If we want them to bleed we have to hemorrhage." He does just that when it comes to leading. He has no greater joy than to help others be the best leader they can be. And I for one am a better leader because of him.

I've noticed through my forty years of ministry that for some leadership is a science. They can tell you the facts, interpret the data, catalogue the principles, and recite current bibliographies of the best out there on leadership. But they don't lead, or even worse, they can't. There is some weird disconnect between the science and the application. This incongruency has always puzzled me. In fact, it has made me distrustful of those who talk the most about leadership. That is, until I met Jimmy in 2005.

When I became his pastor, he became my friend and mentor. Though he didn't have to, he did. And I am better because of it. From the very beginning of my time at First Baptist Orlando, Jimmy was there walking with me to lead a church who had been blessed by many faithful pastors in its 146-year history. As he did, I noticed a passion to develop leaders both among our members as well as our called staff. We began to dream together about more ways we could build leaders at First Baptist Orlando.

I asked Jimmy to develop and lead our intern ministry which he did with great delight. I asked him to develop our current staff training and leadership development which he did with excellence. He continued to teach leadership in small group settings and in one-on-one relationships with key leaders. Many of our leaders today at First Baptist Orlando are a direct result of Jimmy's passion and commitment.

So there are those who can talk about it and those who can do it. Jimmy is a wonderful combination of both. In the parable, Jesus tells of the faithful servant who hears, "Well done thou good and faithful servant." Notice he will not hear, "Well said," but rather, "Well done." In this book Jimmy provides the insight to do it in the local church, where it counts the most. This will be a great textbook for those who want practical, relevant, and biblical help to be the best leader they can be. He doesn't just address the public side of a leader but the private too. The greatest challenge of any leader is not leading others, but leading self. Self-leadership is the hardest leadership of all. And this is where this book will really sharpen every leader. Jimmy helps us to be our best as a leader starting with us and our homes. If we can't lead there, we can't lead. Every pastor and church leader needs this book in their library. What a great resource for the local church today to help her be her best for His glory. No matter how big or small your church is, this book works for you. Because after all, "It's all about leadership."

Thank you Jimmy for leading well. And thank you for taking me along with you. We have laughed together, and we have cried together. Most of all we have led together! Honored to be your pastor.

-Dr. David Uth
Senior Pastor
First Baptist Orlando
Orlando, FL

Becoming a Leader Worth Following...

Psalm 78:72

A Psalm of Asaph

And David shepherded them with integrity of heart;

with skillful hands he led them.

Everything rises and falls on leadership.
– John Maxwell

Introduction

It's All About Leadership

When you read, "It's All about Leadership," what comes to mind? What is "It's"? Perhaps a better question is, "What's NOT about leadership?" Essentially, all arenas and segments of society are impacted by leadership including family, work, education, government, politics, sports, military, church, and even your own life. If this is not true, then intentionally poorly lead and see how that works. The results are usually disastrous.

A leader worth following makes everyone and everything better. In this book, we are going to take a look at what makes someone a leader worth following. Is it title, position, personality, etc.? Though they have a role, they are not what makes someone a leader worth following.

The purpose of this book is to assist people in enhancing their abilities to positively influence whatever part of the world God has entrusted to them, including self, family, friends, co-workers, and beyond. This book has two parts—first, becoming a leader worth following; secondly, developing and using the skills the leader worth following must possess.

First, Asaph writes in Psalm78:72a, "David shepherded them [connection] with integrity of heart [character]."

Second, we read, "...with skillful hands [competency] he led them." (Psalm 78:72b).

Therefore, leaders worth following embody three essential components:

- **Integrity of heart**—authentic character.
- **Skillful hands**—exceptional competency.
- **Shepherding heart**—relational connections.

This book can be used for self-study or for group study. The discovery questions at the end of each chapter are intended to generate helpful dialogue. Also, videos and listening guides of most of this material are available at www.JandLMinistry.com/leadership.

Leadership doesn't just make a difference; it IS the difference. This is especially true of those leaders worth following. In these pages, you and I are going to take a leadership journey together through what makes someone a leader worth following. Get a pen, pencil, or highlighter and write notes in the margin. Dog-ear pages that speak the most to you. Wrestle with the principles. When you're ready, turn the page and better understand why *It's All about Leadership*!

Chapter 1

Understanding Leadership

The more you know about leadership, the faster you grow as a leader and the farther you are able to go as a leader.
- Andy Stanley

In the fall of 2010, The Center for Public Leadership out of Harvard published the results of a study done about the condition of leadership in our country. That poll concluded that 70 percent of the American public believes that we are a nation that is in a leadership crisis. Available data since 2010 indicates this is a consistent percentage.

What words would you use to describe the political, governmental, and institutional condition of leadership in our country: poor, dismal, self-serving, divided, power hungry, power driven, hypocritical, greedy? There's no doubt that it's lacking. It's not always been that way though. If you go back to the Revolutionary War and the birth of our nation when we were a country of two to three million people, I could ask you to name men and women that provided exemplary, difference-making leadership, and we could do that quite readily. We could start with names like Jefferson, Washington, Adams, Franklin and Susan B. Anthony.

Today, with one hundred times the population of Colonial America, where are the exemplary, difference-making, worth-following leaders? There should be a multitude, but it would be a struggle to create a long list. Nevertheless, I am convinced there are many good, even great, leaders out there in every sector of our society. Why are they so hard to find? Perhaps, in a media-crazed world it is not the good who get recognized. Rather, it is the negative and sensational who receive all the coverage. Sadly, bad press sells in the eroding culture. Maybe great leaders are hard to find because they are busy serving others, adding value, and just too humble to seek recognition. Another valid reason could be that the marketplace and the educational systems are motivated to improve the weak as the path to success. We'd be much better off to look for the good and develop it to be great. Great leaders are usually worth following.

So, why are good leaders important? What are we missing if we're missing good leaders? Good leadership provides vision, direction, motivation, and inspiration. Excellent leaders have a capacity to move, empower, and impact people. They know what motivates, inspires, and causes people to want to move forward.

Without good leadership, everybody will go in different directions and there will be a lot of chaos. Leaders help solve problems, and provide encouragement, support, protection, and security for their followers. Situations, people, and process are all improved when there is effective leadership in place.

So, if the ultimate effectiveness of my personal life, the lives of others, vision, direction, motivation, drive, change, problem solving, encouragement, security, success, and support are all determined by good leadership, then what can we do to become more effective as leaders?

How good am I at influencing others?
What is my willingness to do what is necessary to get the job done?

Where these two merge is your measure of effectiveness. Let's say you're about a "one" on the leadership ability scale, but you are willing to work hard and put in the hours to do whatever you need to do to get the job done. What is likely to be your measure of effectiveness as a leader?

You see, there's only two ways to increase your effectiveness. You either work harder or you work smarter. The only problem with working harder is that the older you get the less energy and stamina you have, so you are probably heading for burnout.

Working smarter involves getting wiser and that's improving your leadership ability. That means you have to be willing to change. Your leadership ability impacts your influence, your effectiveness, and your success.

"HOW CAN A LEADER BE MORE EFFECTIVE?"

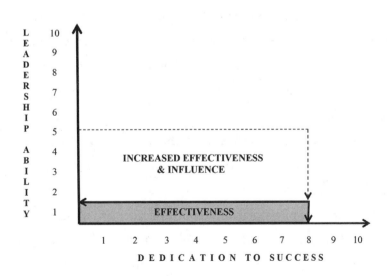

God's leaders are appointed, influenced, and sent! To discover the most effective way to improve your leadership ability, consider what our Lord did in selecting and training His twelve disciples. The principle elements that define what leadership is and does are there in what Jesus did to prepare them to carry on once He was not physically with them. In Mark 3:14 it says, "Jesus appointed twelve (whom He also named apostles) so that they might be with Him and He might send them out to preach."

Jesus appointed twelve men with the express purpose of being a direct influence in the lives of others. Influence can be positive or negative. Influence is the capacity to affect people in their behavior, attitudes, and actions. It is to have an impact on their lives.

Positive influence is what I call a *connected influence* where we connect with people for the right reasons and the right purpose. It is to make a difference, to add value, to give direction, to motivate, to inspire, to drive change, to prevent chaos, and help them to solve problems in their lives. Then there's negative influence where instead of empowering people, leaders are overpowering, intimidating, controlling, and micro-managing them. Followers are doing what their leaders want them to do out of fear that there will be some negative repercussion if they don't do what is demanded of them. Jesus, of course, was a leader with the mindset of positively influencing His disciples and equipping them to be productive in the Kingdom business.

A leader is a positive influence in the lives of those he is called to lead. Jesus appointed the twelve and called them apostles to be with Him, under His positive influence so He could then send them out to preach. Jesus had a specific purpose in mind for this leadership training. He took them with Him into the field so He could later release them into that field to go and do even more than He did during His earthly ministry.

A leader is a person who influences people to accomplish a purpose. Jesus' leadership influenced His disciples to change their world after His death. All those who influence others to change their attitudes and actions are leaders no matter their title or age.

Case in point, our two-year-old grandson. Our daughter and her husband had to be out of town for a few days and we were babysitting our two grandsons. One was two years old and the other was ten years old. Now, you would think the ten-year-old would be the leader, but it became very obvious who the real leader of the pack was. The two-year-old grabbed my finger and said, "Come on, Daddy Jim." Next thing I know, I'm on my hands and knees crawling into an opening in a train that's meant for someone the size of a two-year-old. Then he went to my wife and said, "Come on, Mama Lou." Then he went to his big brother and said, "Come on, Tyler." Next thing we know we have two adults and one ten-year-old in a train that was built to hold two-year-olds. He was leading. He influenced each of us to get into that train with him. You think that a two-year old can't be a leader? They do it in our homes all the time. It happens every moment of every day. You put two children in a sandbox and one of them will lead and the other will follow.

Ken Blanchard said, "Leadership is a process of influence. Anytime you seek to influence the thinking, behavior, and development of people toward accomplishing a goal in their personal or professional lives, you are taking on the role of a leader."

Warren Buffett said, "A leader is someone who can get things done through other people."

A leader is relational and directional. In Mark 3:14, Jesus appointed the twelve to be with Him. That's relational. He then sent them out to preach with a specific purpose, reason, goal, and objective. That's directional. If leadership is about taking people with you, then leadership first of all is about building a relationship. Do you want people to follow you because they have to or because they want to? Do we want our wives to follow and be submissive to a husband's leadership in a home just because they have to? It ought to be because we're worth following. That's what really matters. Just giving somebody a title as leader of the home doesn't mean they're worth following.

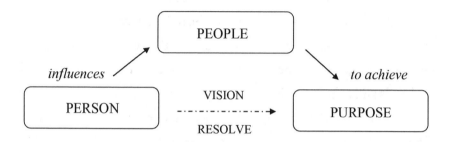

A Leader Is Worth Following

In order to be a leader worth following, one needs vision. A leader has to know where he or she is going. Then a leader has to have the determination, grit, and perseverance to stay on a path that leads to fulfilling that vision. One of the things that makes us different as Christian leaders is that we have a relationship with Jesus Christ. The twelve disciples of Jesus had a relationship with Him that gave them a chance to learn the godly way to handle leadership.

So, the focus of this book will be identifying and incorporating into our leadership style the distinctive characteristics of Christian leadership. There are many people in the world who lead and influence the behavior of others who are not Christians. People like you and me, who say we have a relationship with Christ, should emulate His distinct leadership qualities, not those of the world. Should the fact that you and I have a relationship with Jesus Christ make a difference in how we affect, influence, and impact others compared to the unsaved person who may be a moral and ethical person but does not have that relationship with Him? The answer is *yes* because there are very significant differences between the two.

One very important difference has to do with how we handle the authority we are given as leaders. One thing that makes us unique as Christian leaders is that because we are followers of Jesus Christ, we are under His banner and authority. Since we are surrendered to Him, He is the one calling the shots in our lives. He is our authority. In Mark 16, Jesus told the disciples that He had personally influenced and impacted them and that God the Father had given Him all authority. Now, He was sending them out with that same authority. As His disciples, we have that same authority as well.

We also have a unique standard we live by. Our worldview is different. We have God's written Word as our manual for living. He has given us very specific directions on how to live a godly life which will directly affect our leadership style. Our standard of conduct for our daily living, both at home and at work, is based on God's Word, His way, and His purpose.

Although this should directly affect our worldview, unfortunately, Barna research indicates that less than 10 percent of evangelical Christians actually consistently live with a biblically Christian worldview in both their homes and places of employment. Many Christians have developed a double standard saying it is the only way they can survive in the real world, which is expressly warned against in the Word of God.

We are told to be in the world but not of the world. We are told to renew our minds daily and not be conformed to the world though we are called to influence the world for Christ. We are also assured that though it may seem impossible to man to live the godly life, He has equipped us to do so, saying, "What seems impossible for man is indeed possible for God" (Luke 18:27).

Our motive for who we are and what we do is different than non-Christian leaders. We're here to please Jesus and glorify God. We honor Him at work and at home and glorify God in everything we say and do. We are to succeed as God defines success, exemplifying the benefits of serving the God of the universe, being who God created us to be, and doing what He designed us to do.

Our whole motivation as a leader is to be a witness for Him in the marketplace every day at work. It really has nothing to do with a paycheck. Yes, you need a paycheck to pay the bills and to have some quality of life. God has invested in you, resourced you, and given you education, opportunity, and a paycheck so you can rub shoulders with people who need to hear and know about Jesus. You're not an employee or employer, a professional or business person first. You're a Christian first and foremost. By virtue of God's image in your life, you are uniquely positioned as an engineer, an architect or an IT guy so you can influence the world in your sphere of influence. We get in trouble and we lose our influence when we don't realize that.

Next, we have a unique power available in our lives to influence those around us with a positive influence. We have the power of the Holy Spirit operating in our lives that the unsaved person doesn't have. We can tap into this power and He will show us things and guide us around obstacles which gives us a distinct advantage over our unsaved counter parts if we will just trust and listen to His promptings. We go to work each day with the Spirit of God within us, connecting us with the mind of Christ and the wisdom from above. What a powerful resource God has given us, yet we often live as if He doesn't exist.

So many times, we fall back on our own strength and trust in ourselves instead of Him until we get ourselves so bogged down in the world that we wonder how God could have let these things happen to us. Yes, too often our work is all about me, myself, and I, instead of, "What do You want me to do today, God?" When things are difficult at work or we are persecuted, we wonder *why us* instead of *what does God want* accomplished through this experience. The Word of God clearly instructs us to acknowledge Him in all of our ways, and He will make our paths straight. There is no greater power to influence our world as salt and light than having the Creator of the Universe giving us guidance, direction, and tools to bring His truth to our troubled world. He's right here with us each and every day, every step of the way.

Entitlement or Servant Leadership

Our whole model for living is different than that of the world around us. There are two basic mindsets toward life—entitlement or servant leadership. The entitlement mindset says, "I'm entitled, I deserve, I have my rights, I've got my position, and I deserve my perks." Jesus was clear that His style of leadership was based on a servant-leadership mindset.

As Christians, we're in the servant business. That's who we are and what we do. Any other mindset is entitlement. The world functions with an entitlement mindset. We don't want to be like them. We are not to look like them, act like them, or talk like them. They should never doubt what and Who it is we stand for especially in the marketplace and in our communities. We should be actively leading in whatever capacity God has placed us as we exemplify servant leadership just as our Lord and Savior showed us.

God has also blessed us with spiritual gifts. He has uniquely designed each one of us with the personality and the spiritual gifting to accomplish His purpose for us. God gives infinite wisdom and supernaturally endows His children to be more effective in leadership, administration, and management. We are each responsible for discovering and developing whatever God has placed within us to achieve His goal and purpose for us. He has given us a vision that is attainable for us, but not without His supernatural assistance.

If we take all of these unique distinctive characteristics that make us Christians and boil them down to one word, it is Christ-likeness. We are to be like Christ when we seek to influence others. That means that we're striving in our spiritual development as a follower of Christ to have the attitudes and behaviors that are modeled after Him. Barna did research on those who claim to be followers of Christ, yet when they were asked to define what it meant to be a Christian, I'm sad to report that approximately only 14 percent consistently aligned their living with the attitudes and behaviors of Jesus Christ.

No wonder the world ignores us. We are to be a peculiar people. We are to be like Christ. Even if they do not understand that we are emulating Christ, they should see there is something very different about us. They should see such a positive difference that they want to know what it is and why.

Henry Blackaby said, "Spiritual leadership is not an occupation, it's a calling."

Christian business people, physicians, educators, politicians, and parents all ought to be spiritual leaders. More and more people in secular occupations are taking their calling as spiritual leaders seriously and they are impacting the world and expanding God's Kingdom.

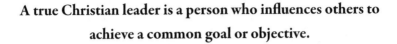

A true Christian leader is a person who influences others to achieve a common goal or objective.

Charles Swindoll wrote: "Leadership is not optional; it is essential. Essential for motivation and direction. Essential for evaluation and accomplishment. It is the one ingredient essential for the success of any organization. Take away leadership and it isn't long before confusion replaces vision. Volunteers or employees who once dedicated themselves to their tasks begin to drift without leadership. Morale erodes. Enthusiasm fades. The whole system finally grinds to a halt. Peter Drucker's famous line is both timeless and true: 'If an enterprise fails to perform, we rightly hire, not different workers, but a new president.' When there's trouble brewing at the bottom, chances are good that a major part of the problem is at the top. Whether the scene is business, industry, labor, government, education, athletics, military, religion, or domestic, the hope and progress of the organization rests in the hands of those who are in charge."

QUESTIONS FOR SELF-REFLECTION
CHAPTER ONE—UNDERSTANDING LEADERSHIP

1. *What is your definition of a leader?*

2. *What do you think about Jimmy's simple definition of leadership drawn from Mark 3:14, "A leader is a person who influences people to achieve a purpose?"*

3. *Would you agree that leadership is largely about earning and exerting influence on people?*

4. *What do you think about Jesus describing a leader worth following as a servant (Luke 22:24-27)?*

5. *How would life be different if we all modeled servant leadership?*

6. *What was your best learning from this chapter and how can you apply it today?*

Chapter 2

Developing Leadership

Every time you improve your ability to lead, your life becomes more effective and your influence becomes deeper and greater in the lives of others. It can be as simple as a conversation with another leader or reading a chapter in a book. Whatever you do to develop yourself impacts the development of other leaders. When you look at the life of somebody who has impacted your life like your mom, dad, grandparent, coach, teacher, boss, or friend, what is it about that person that you want to be like?

The Gallup Organization did a survey of 10-15,000 followers and asked: What are you looking for in someone that you want to follow? There were hundreds and hundreds of answers, but here are the top four that stood out front.

- *They want people they can trust that are authentic, honest, and have integrity.*
- *They want people that show compassion; that care about them and are genuinely interested in them as a person and not as if they are a commodity to get something done for them or for the organization.*

- *They want a leader who provides stability, somebody that gives them a sense of security so they don't have to go to work every day wondering, "Will I be here tomorrow?"*
- *They want a leader to give them a reason for doing what they're doing, to see that what they do matters, and a reason to keep going.*

The first one is by far the front runner. A leader needs to emulate a sense of credibility, trustworthiness, reliability, integrity, and honesty. Often the others fall into place when a leader has these attributes.

If this is what folks are saying they want in their leaders, are we doing that? Are we living those things? If we aspire to make a difference with our lives, we've got to make sure these attributes are emulated in our lives.

Are leaders born or are they developed?

If you had asked me that question years ago, I would have answered that it's probably 90 percent innate and the rest can be developed. Having been a serious student of leadership for many years, and having watched hundreds of people in this process, I've come to new conclusions. I now believe that 25-30 percent is innate and the rest of it is developed. Leading others well is a skill that anyone can learn and practice if one chooses to develop it.

Anyone can be a really good leader if he learns the right skill sets in order to become more effective and more influential.

Psalm 78:72 is my life verse on leadership. In Psalm 78:70-72, Asaph says, "David shepherded them with integrity of heart, with skillful hands he led them." Notice the last three words, "he led them." He was a leader in Asaph's mind. What oxygen is to our body, credibility is to leadership.

We've got to be trustworthy, reliable, credible, honest, and have integrity. These are what would make others want to follow you or me.

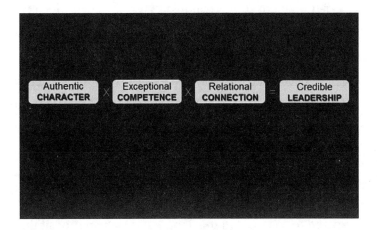

David is our example. He had authentic character, exceptional competence, and was relational. He shepherded them with integrity of heart and with skillful hands. That means exceptional competence. He was somebody who knew what he was doing. He connected with people and built relationships. Anything we do to improve our character and to be more like Christ is upping our credibility whether with our spouse, our kids, our co-workers, our friends, or our boss. Whenever we're building meaningful relationships, we are not using people because we genuinely care about them. This also increases our credibility as a leader.

We've each got to decide which of these we need more work on improving. As we move forward, we're going to spend a chapter on authentic character, looking at flaws and then trying to get them repaired. Then we will discuss what makes for exceptional competence; knowing what to do, how to do it, and getting it done. Then we will spend time on the importance of building and investing in meaningful, caring, and compassionate relationships. I believe these are the three big rocks that make for credible leadership.

Henry Blackaby has written one of the greatest books on spiritual leadership. He said,

"Society's problem is more than just a lack of leaders. Society's great deficit is that it does not have enough leaders who understand and practice Christian principles of leadership." Effective leaders are not enough. The world needs people in business that know how to apply their faith in the board room as well as in the Bible Study room. We need Christian leaders who know God, and how to lead, and understand and practice Christian principles of leadership. They lead in a Christian manner which will be phenomenally more effective in their world than even the most skilled and qualified leaders who lead without God. Spiritual leadership is not restricted to pastors and missionaries. It is the responsibility of all Christians whom God wants to use to make a difference in the world.

The challenge for today's leaders is to discern the difference between the latest leadership fads and timeless truths established by God.

When Asaph observed David's life, he outlined three critical components to be a leader worth following. Why should anyone let you lead them and have influence in their life? Because you have a title, hold a position, have a strong personality, exude great charisma? There is more, so much more to be a leader worth following. The fact that people follow you is not necessarily an indicator that you deserve to be followed. There is a big difference between having a following and being worth following. Asaph provides great insight into what makes a person worth following as a leader. When these are present, credibility is generated and influence is permitted.

In the next three chapters, I will take an in-depth look at each of these essential components to be a leader worth following: authentic character, exceptional competency and relational connection.

QUESTIONS FOR SELF-REFLECTION
CHAPTER TWO—DEVELOPING LEADERSHIP

1. *What are your thoughts on the unending debate over whether leaders are born or made?*

2. *What attitudes and behaviors generate credibility that opens the door to have influence on people?*

3. *Why should anyone let you have influence and lead them?*

4. *Can you think of people you have permitted to gain influence in your life? Why did you extend them this special privilege?*

5. *How do you feel about Gallup's research indicating why we allow people to have influence in our lives (trust, compassion, stability, and hope)?*

6. *Generally speaking, do you agree that authentic character, exceptional competency, and relational connection are key components to being a leader worth following? Are there other key components to consider?*

7. *What was your best learning from this chapter and how can you apply it today?*

Chapter 3

The Character of a Leader Worth Following

The greatest crisis in the world today is a crisis in leadership.
And the greatest crisis in leadership is a crisis in character.
—Howard Hendricks

Leadership that matters, leadership that's credible, leadership that makes a difference is character driven above everything else. It's far more important than everything else in our lives, yet we live in a world where leadership is more about talent, competency, personality and charisma.

Bernard Madoff, Jerry Sandusky, Lindsay Lohan, and Manti Te'o are a few names that have one thing in common. They're all celebrities, but they all also had flawed characters.

Peter Drucker said, "Quality of character doesn't make a leader, but lack of it flaws the entire process."

So what is character? It's not as easy to define as one might think, but we know it when we see it. We know it when we're around it. So, when we say someone has character, what is it that they have? Some of the answers that might come to mind are integrity, trustworthiness, self-discipline, fairness, dependability, and consistency.

> *Better to be poor and walk in **integrity** than to be crooked in one's ways even though rich.*
> (Proverbs 28:6)

The word *character* is not found in the Old Testament. There's a concept related to character which is found about twenty-five times. The Hebrew word *tôm* means *to be a force, to have impact.*

That's exactly what character does. It's a force, an influence, and has impact on others.

When you look in the New Testament, *character* is mentioned twice in Romans 5:3-4. Paul talks about how suffering produces endurance, endurance produces character, and character produces hope. The word used for *character* means *to engrave or to etch.* Every time we choose an attitude or a behavior, whether we know it or not, we are etching or drawing a picture of our character. Character is the sum total of a person's emotional, spiritual, and psychological qualities. These distinct qualities, both good and bad, reflect who we are and what we do regardless of the circumstances.

Andy Stanley, author of *Next Generation Leader* and *Louder Than Words*, says, "Character is the will to do what's right as defined by God regardless of personal cost."

Thomas Macaulay said, "The measure of a man's real character is what he would do if he knew he would never be found out."

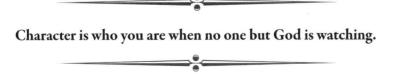

Character is who you are when no one but God is watching.

Character clears the conscience. Proverbs 10:9 says, "Whoever walks in integrity walks securely." People who have character can sleep at night. People who have character don't have to have perfect memories. If you're going to lie, you've got to remember everything you've said.

> *One who walks in **integrity** will be safe,*
> *but whoever follows crooked ways will fall into the Pit.*
> (Proverbs 28:18)

Character produces hope. We all face suffering, trials, and difficulty in our life's journey. Suffering is what produces endurance and perseverance which is staying power. We can't always control what happens to us, but we can control how we respond to it. When we respond to the difficulty in the right way and endurance permeates our lives, character is being etched in us. It is character that produces the hope and the confidence that we will make it through any difficult time.

Character builds trust. People of character are reliable, honest, and we can lean on them. We can believe in them. Character strengthens relationships. The strongest relationship we can build in our life is with God. When we have a strong and intimate relationship with Him, we can make it through anything we face in this life and we can be the leaders He has called us to be.

Who Can Come into God's Presence?

Lord, who may dwell in Your sanctuary? Who may live on Your holy hill? He who walks blamelessly; he who does what is righteous; he who speaks the truth from the heart; has no slander on his tongue; who does his neighbor no wrong; who casts no slur on his fellow man; who despises

*a vile man, but honors those who fear the Lord; who keeps his oath
even when it hurts; who lends his money without interest and does not
accept a bribe against the innocent.*
(Psalm 15:1-2)

Psalm 15:1-5 is a tremendous passage that provides us with a litany of
the marks of someone with character. It begins by asking who can come
into God's presence and build the most intimate relationship with Him.
The requirements then listed are marks of character. Those who have these
marks consistently in their lives are the ones who have a deep, intimate
relationship with Him. My favorite phrase is at the very end of this passage.

He who does these things will never be shaken.
(Psalm 15:5b)

What a promise! Do you want to live an unshakable life regardless
of what comes into your life? Then be a person of character which gives
stamina and strength in your life.

*A good name is to be chosen rather than great riches and
favor is better than silver or gold.*
(Proverbs 22:1)

A good name is character. If the magic wand were to be waved and you
had the choice of great riches or great character what would you choose?
The writer of Proverbs says choose the character.

*As a pastor, I spend a great deal of my time digging people out
of personal catastrophes. Events that were often years in the making*

which somehow in their mind caught them by surprise. A broken marriage. An unwanted pregnancy. A financial crisis. Problems at work. As I listen, two questions race through my mind.

Why is it that we have such a difficult time recognizing the traps we lay for ourselves?

What could this person have done to avoid this situation?

The answer almost always seems to boil down to the same issue. Character.

Compromised convictions. Reshuffled values. Selfishness. Somewhere these individuals veered off the path of rightness, but nothing happened at first. At least nothing they were aware of. This was the beginning of their personal slag heap and it stood within striking distance of their souls. There's another group of people with whom I interface on a regular basis. Those who are facing the inevitable storms of life that are not of their own making. Storms that have been created by the character deficits of others. That is true.

- Andy Stanley

I read that and thought, *you know I've been a Christian for a long time and I've been in full-time ministry a good bit of that life.* Looking back over the hundreds and hundreds of people that have approached me, met with me, and talked with me, whether it was personal issues, marital issues, or vocational issues, in many of those instances they got themselves there because of a character deficit. I'm convinced that every divorce is a result of a character deficit either in the husband or the wife or both.

In all probability, every relationship that gets strained in life is because one of us at that moment in time is having some character issues. It could be selfishness on our part. It could be demanding our own rights. Whatever the case may be, character deficiency is what causes the problem.

So, let's answer Andy Stanley's questions and begin to prevent these storms that are of our own making.

Why is it we have such a difficult time recognizing the traps we lay for ourselves?
What can we do to avoid these preventable situations in our lives?
What are the character deficits in our lives we need to rectify?

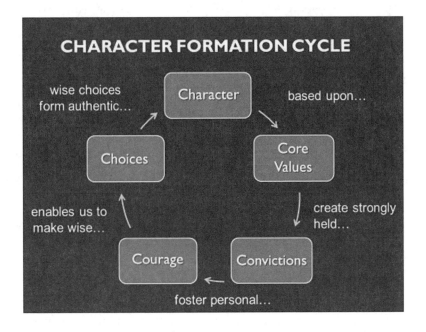

The Core Values of Character

When wealth is lost, nothing is lost.
When health is lost, something is lost.
When character is lost, all is lost.
– Billy Graham

If character is that important, where does it come from? What are the origins of authentic, biblical, godly, Jesus-like character? Are we born with it? If we are, then why do some of the godliest parents end up with some of the most ungodly kids? Why do kids who grew up in basically godless homes become great people of character? It's because the only way to attain such character is to build it and develop it. Our goal is to be more like Jesus in attitude, belief, and behavior, but it does not happen accidentally. We must choose to take charge of who we are and what we do.

In Luke 6:43-45, Jesus said, "No good tree bears bad fruit, nor again does a bad tree bear good fruit, for each tree is known by its own fruit. For figs are not gathered from thorn bushes, nor are grapes picked from a bramble bush. The good person out of the good treasure of his heart produces good, and the evil person out of his evil treasure produces evil, for out of the abundance of the heart his mouth speaks."

Our character is always changing; maybe for the better, maybe for the worse, but it's never static. The danger is to think that the good character of today is good enough for late tonight when sitting in front of the computer and temptation comes across the screen. It's a continual process. We can't live on character achievements of the past and think it will get us through in the future. It's a day by day choice.

If we're after Christ-like, godly character, we need to understand what Christ-like character is and how to develop it in order to make the right choices.

Core Values

Our character is based on our personal core values. The beliefs that are most important to us determine our choice of attitudes and actions moment by moment, day by day, and week by week. Core values create strongly held convictions. A conviction is something that has a hold of us. It filters everything we say and do. When we have convictions, they enable us and foster personal courage. Character requires courage. Courage enables us to make wise choices. Every time we make a wise, godly choice, we have just etched another groove in our character.

We all have core values. The most derelict of humans, every person in prison has core values. The person in the highest office at the most incredibly profitable company has core values. A six-year old has core values. The sad thing is, though they are profoundly powerful, most of us have never ever thought about our personal core values and convictions. When we're young, our core values tend to be handed to us by parents, teachers, and coaches. As we move into the teenage years and early twenties, our core values are more peer-driven. In many ways, what happens today is the media and the culture we live in determine our core values. Before we know it, we get softened and we end up saying things, doing things, and going places we never would if we thought about what our biblically-based convictions ought to be.

Are the core values I have what God wants me to have?
If I have godly core values, do I really live that way?
Is there a gap between what I want the core values to be before God and how I actually live and choose in terms of attitudes and actions on a day by day basis?

It's that gap that can get us in trouble in our character, compromise our integrity, and cause people to lose trust in us as leaders. It's that gap that weakens our relationships. Appendix 1 (p. 183) has a helpful exercise for identifying your personal core values.

*The righteous walk in **integrity**— happy are the children who follow them!*
(Proverbs 20:7)

Integrity

I did not sit down and deliberately pray through the core values I thought God wanted me to live by until I was forty-nine years old. However, I have tried to live with the same core values intentionally ever since then. Those core values are truth according to the Word of God, integrity, excellence, and responsibility. Integrity is real in my life. I don't just say it, I live it. I am faithful and consistent in what I do.

Integrity is a term from the mathematical world. Do you remember what an integer is? It's not just a number. It's a whole number. It's not fractionalized, not parted. People of character are whole people. There's an integration between what they say and what they do. There's no veneer in their lives. They're the real deal wherever they are and whoever they're with, whatever it costs. What you see is what you get. They are who they are because they're people of integrity. Billy Graham said, "Integrity is the glue that holds our way of life together."

True instruction was in his mouth, and no wrong was found on his lips.
*He walked with me in **integrity** and uprightness, and he turned many*
from iniquity.
(Malachi 2:6 emphasis added)

Integrity is not necessary if your aspirations as a leader end with simply persuading people to follow you. Can you be an effective leader and not be a person of character? Yes, just not one worth following. However, if at the end of the day your intent is for those who follow you to respect you, integrity is a must. Your accomplishments as a leader will make your name known. Your character will determine what people associate with your name. Your competency, your ability to do what you do well, will open some doors for you but it's your character that will determine how you act when you walk through that door.

Integrity moves you to strive for excellence which means:

- *I do not settle for the status quo.*
- *I do not do just enough to get by.*
- *I strive to do and be the best I can possibly be.*
- *I take ownership and responsibility for my life.*

If you can, find someone that will be honest with you, ask them if they know what your core values are. See if they match the four you wrote down. You could be surprised.

> *The Lord judges the peoples;*
> *judge me, O Lord, according to my righteousness*
> *and according to the **integrity** that is in me.*
> (Psalm 7:8 emphasis added)

Job was a man who walked in integrity in the face of great tribulation. "Until I die I will not put away my **integrity** from me" (Job 27:5 emphasis added). Take the time to read the whole book of Job, but consider carefully what God said about this man of integrity.

> *The Lord said to Satan, "Have you considered my servant Job? There is no one like him on the earth, a blameless and upright man who fears God and turns away from evil. He still persists in his **integrity**, although you incited me against him, to destroy him for no reason."*
> (Job 2:3 emphasis added)

Wouldn't we like to have God speak this way about us as well? To attain such status with God, we must discover where we may have character flaws. Please stop here and take the time to go through the worksheet provided in Appendix 2 (p. 185) that will help you address integrity issues in your life. It will begin to identify where some of the chinks or gaps in your character may be hiding. Then you can move forward and begin to deal with character flaws.

Where Is My Character Flawed?

Any time a leader neglects to repair flaws in his character the flaws become
worse and inevitably lead to a downward spiral
culminating in the destruction of a leader's moral foundation.
Leaders cannot escape who they truly are and what they do
in the dark comes to light.
- John Maxwell

As you went through the worksheet, you probably discovered a character flaw. There are a few names we have come across in the Bible that will help us define some specific character flaws even in our heroes of faith. Abraham lied more than once. He just couldn't live with the truth. Moses had an anger issue which resulted in murder. David had an issue with lust that lead to all kinds of other issues in his life. Peter dealt with pride, self-control, and arrogance issues.

We've all got chinks in our armor. What happens over time is we learn to justify and to live with them. We tend to cover them up to some degree, but if we are really honest with ourselves, we know we have them and make excuses like, "Well, it's just the way I am, it could be worse, or at least I'm not like so and so." Having learned to justify these character flaws, we give them permission to remain in our thoughts, feelings, and actions.

The Battle with Self

Psychotherapist, Sheldon Kopp, believes all the significant battles in life are waged within self. As we examine ourselves, we discover what those battles are. We have two choices. First, we can be like the man who visited his doctor and found out that he had serious health issues. When the doctor showed him his x-ray and told him he needed painful and expensive surgery, the patient replied, "Okay, doc, but how much would you charge me just to touch up the x-ray?"

Have you touched up your x-rays? Have you lived with your character flaw for ten, fifteen or twenty years? Maybe you've confessed it over and over again because of the condemning nature of guilt, yet you still battle it. Why haven't you been able to gain the victory? Maybe it is because you have just touched up the x-rays instead of submitting to the needed surgery.

Fame is a vapor.
Popularity is an accident.
Money takes wings.
The only thing that endures is character.
- Horace Greeley

There is a way out, though. Your second choice is to ask for God's help. First, define the flaw requiring refinement. What is your signature sin; where do you most struggle with temptation? Then determine how the flaw has been maintained. You've got to dig down deep with the help of the Holy Spirit and ask yourself, *Why do I keep justifying it and blaming everyone else?*

Next, decide what you desire to become and set manageable and achievable short-term goals. Then it is critical that you disclose your flaw to an accountability partner. If you're not willing to confess it, then it enslaves you, controls you, paralyzes you, and owns you. Be selective in who you tell, but get it out in the open.

Depend on the power of the Holy Spirit. Paul said in Romans 8:11 that the same power that raised Jesus Christ from the dead that first Easter morning lives in every one of us as His child. Lastly, develop your spiritual walk. Spiritual growth leads to character change. Change is never comfortable, but change can create more Christ-likeness in us by the power of the Holy Spirit in our attitudes, our behaviors, our actions, and our beliefs.

> *The only thing that walks back from the tomb with the mourners and refuses to be buried is the character of a man.*
> – J. R. Miller

The Diamond Ring

Back in the late '90s, Linda and I made our way over to a local mall near our home. Linda wanted to do some shopping. I'm a buyer not a shopper, so like most men after about fifteen minutes I needed caffeine intravenously administered into my body. All the life and energy had been sucked out of me and I needed to sit down. So, I bought a cup of coffee and sat down on the bench just kind of watching people.

When I finished the coffee, I got up and walked into one of the jewelry stores near where I was sitting. I walked up to the counter and told the lady I'd like to see the most expensive diamond ring they had. When she asked me why, I told her I was not interested in buying, I just wanted to see it. So, she did what I would have done, she went and got the manager. When I told him what I wanted, they commiserated after a second and then he went back to the vault, brought it out, opened it up, and I looked at it. It was beautiful. I just looked at it for several minutes, then I went out, and sat down to wait for Linda to finish her shopping.

As I began to study this character issue, God brought that experience back to my remembrance. What I realized is that when I held that expensive ring in my hand, the only thing I looked at was the jewel. However, it is the strength and quality of the setting that determines the security of the diamond. That diamond represents everything we hold dear and precious in our lives like our spouses, our kids, our work, etc.

The ring's setting is our character. If the setting gets weak, it's just a matter of time before we forfeit the diamond. If you knew the setting on that expensive diamond ring was flawed, why wouldn't you protect it by fixing the flaw?

Unfortunately, like sometimes happens with a diamond ring, we don't know the setting is weak and flawed until it's too late and we lose what was precious. We are fortunate because we have just discovered our character is in need of repair. Now that we know, we can begin to fix it. If we don't, there may be a price to pay that we really do not want to pay. It is this quality and strength of our character that protects all that is valuable and precious in our lives.

QUESTIONS FOR SELF-REFLECTION
CHAPTER THREE—CHARACTER

1. *How essential is character to leadership?*

2. *When a person has character exactly what is it that he has?*

3. *What makes character important?*

4. *How do you respond to the quotes by Billy Graham and Andy Stanley?*

5. *When you think of someone you know who has character, who comes to mind and why?*

6. *What was your best learning from this chapter and how can you apply it today?*

7. *What are your greatest character strengths and weaknesses?*

8. *What are your thoughts on Jimmy's character formation cycle?*

9. *What are your core values?*

10. *What character flaws need your attention?*

11. *What did you learn from Jimmy's ring story?*

Chapter 4

The Competency of a Leader Worth Following

Like me, you are probably inspired by top performance and high achievers whether it's in the sports world, the marketplace, or academics. Out of His goodness, God has richly resourced all of us to be able to do a few things remarkably well. Then when you came to Christ, you received added resources spiritually to be able to do a few things exceptionally well as you make the right choices.

Psalm 78:72 says, "David shepherded them with integrity of heart and with skillful hands he led them." He led with exceptional competency. There are a number of passages in both the Old Testament and the New Testament that speak to this concept of the skill and ability God has invested in us.

Then bring near to you Aaron your brother, and his sons with him, from among the people of Israel, to serve me as priests—Aaron and Aaron's sons. Nadab and Abihu, Eleazar and Ithamar. And you shall make holy garments for Aaron your brother, for glory and for beauty. You shall speak to

*all **who have ability, whom I have endowed with
an able mind** that they make the garments to
consecrate him for My priesthood.*
(Exodus 28:1-3 emphasis added)

These folks had a unique ability invested in them by God to carry out the needed craft. God invested in these people just like He's invested in you and me in order to do something exceptionally well for Him.

*The Lord said to Moses, "See, I have called by name Bezalel the son of Uri, son of Hur, of the tribe of Judah, and I have filled him with the Spirit of God, with ability and intelligence, with knowledge and all craftsmanship, and he is able to do artistic designs, to work in gold, silver, and bronze, in cutting stones for setting, and in carving wood, to work in every craft. And behold I have appointed with him Ohaliab, the son of Ahisamach, of the tribe of Dan. And **I have given to all able men ability that they may be able to make that which I have commanded you.***
(Exodus 31:1-6 emphasis added)

In the New Testament in the Parable of the Talents, God invested in each one of these servants according to their ability. In 1 Peter 4:10, he writes that as each has received a gift, let him use it faithfully. However, you can't use it if you don't know what it is. If I were to ask you if you know what your greatest asset other than the Holy Spirit is, I hope your answer would be that you are your greatest asset. It is not your wife, not your kids, and not your best friends. You are your greatest asset through the filling and the power of the Holy Spirit in your life.

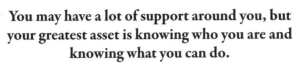

You may have a lot of support around you, but your greatest asset is knowing who you are and knowing what you can do.

Exceptional Competence

Marginal, ordinary, mediocre, satisfactory, common, and average are not words that describe someone who is exceptionally competent. Even though we would never dream of praying and asking God to help us to be ordinary, mediocre, normal, and average, that's where we usually settle.

However, when someone is exceptional, they're described as extraordinary, outstanding, dazzling, captivating, and over the top. Time, energy, and commitment are the price we must pay to be exceptionally competent. The path to get there is hard, but worth the effort.

The subtitle to "Talent is Overrated" asks *"What really separates world class performers from everybody else?"* The book begins with the question, "How do people become world class performers or achievers?" People that are exceptional often say the reason is they simply have more talent to start with and they have just worked harder. Sounds good, but research just doesn't back that up.

It's really not so much about being over-talented and over-achieving that makes anyone exceptionally competent. Obviously, knowing their talents and working hard are a part of it, but those are not the definers.

God wants our skill to be a divinely choreographed ballet. He wants it to be a thing of beauty not of stress. He meant for it to work for good not just for results. He gave us our skill to be used for His glory not ours. Skill matters to God and it should matter to us, too. We cannot be satisfied with mediocrity and still work wholeheartedly unto the Lord. We cannot just get by and still glorify God in all that we do.

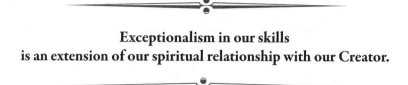

**Exceptionalism in our skills
is an extension of our spiritual relationship with our Creator.**

Skill is not a business necessity, but a spiritual imperative. It has everything to do with our relationship with God and what He's entrusted in us.

Mark 6:3 says, "Is not this the carpenter, the son of Mary and brother of James and Joses and Judas and Simon?" They are talking about Jesus. Our ultimate example of skill is embodied in the life that Jesus lived on this earth. Jesus was skill personified. Luke records that as Jesus grew into a man He was known for His wisdom and abilities. His work gained Him favor not just with God, but with men as well. In other words, Jesus was respected. He was known for excelling. Even at a young age, He had a reputation for skilled work. Long before He began His full-time public ministry, Jesus of Nazareth was a very skilled carpenter.

The word used to describe Jesus in Mark 6:3 is the Greek word *technon*; someone who understood something completely and transformed that knowledge into creations of wonder and excellence. This is someone who was able to take a rough piece of wood and put it into a process of miraculous conversion. Even before He was identified as the Messiah, Jesus was known as a skilled craftsman. *Technon* pictures someone, who with a minimum of technical equipment and a maximum of craftsmanship, could make something beautiful out of very little. Jesus was a master at His craft.

Why was Christ driven to excellence of skill? It was not because He was a perfectionist. It was not because He wanted to dominate the carpentry market in Nazareth or to prove that He had what it takes. For Jesus, doing His best had to do with His spiritual relationship with God. That's a little bit different perspective and really elevates the abilities that we have and how we invest those abilities.

So, someone is exceptionally competent when they know what to do, have the ability to do it, and the discipline to get it done. I've watched a lot of people that have the first two, but then don't have the last one which is the fortitude, the discipline, determination, and the perseverance to get it done. You've got to have all of those components.

Exceptional competency requires what I call great self-awareness. It means having clarity, tremendous insight, and understanding about who you are and how God has crafted you to do something unique and special for Him.

Ben Franklin said, "There are three things extremely hard: steel, diamond, and to know oneself; to really know oneself."

It's hard to know oneself because we get so busy we don't even think about it. We're survivors and are often just trying to get through life. Secondly, it seems to take almost a lifetime to realize we only get one shot at this. That's connected to what we do with the assignment that God has given us.

Our God-given Resources

In Psalm 139:13-16, David writes, "For You God formed my inward parts; You knitted me together in my mother's womb." Now when you think of all of the metaphors or word pictures that the Holy Spirit could have picked to describe how God uniquely crafted every one of us, and He picked knitting. Pretty much a lost art now, but my mother was a knitter.

I remember how painstaking and deliberate it was to knit something for birthdays or for Christmas.

David continues in verse 14, "I praise You for I am fearfully and wonderfully made; wonderful are Your works. My soul knows it full well." The idea here of fearfully and wonderfully really means awesome and amazing. The verb made there means for a reason. In other words, I know I am an awesome and amazing creation that God created for a reason, for a purpose. Most people don't know it full well. We spend too much time caring too much about what others think while caring too little about what God thinks. We find ourselves living 60-80 years of life and not necessarily wasting it, just not wisely investing it.

Then verses 15-16 say, "My frame, [my substance, my life, my strengths, my weaknesses, my talents, my abilities, my personality, everything about me] was not hidden from You when I was made in secret. Intricately woven [knitted], in the depths of the earth. Your eyes saw my unformed substance." God supervised our unformed substance from conception to delivery.

Up to this point we're wonderfully and uniquely crafted by our Creator, the master weaver, but notice how things turn in the second half of verse 16. "In Your book were written, every one of them, the days that were formed for me, when as yet, there were none of them." In other words, You created me, God, a long time before momma and daddy produced me, but You did that for a reason.

You had an end in mind for my life and that's why You made me the way You made me.

Whenever engineers want to create a product, they generally speak to what the end use is going to be and then they create a manufacturing process that meets that end use. However, there is no guarantee when the consumer possesses the item that it will be used for the purpose it was designed to accomplish. For example, how many times have you and I used a pen for a hole punch or a pair of scissors as a screw driver? Is that the optimum use for which these tools were originally designed? Of course not.

The question you have got to answer is, what did God design me to accomplish? He did design you with an end in mind so that your life would have maximum production, effectiveness, and influence for Him. The sooner you discover what that is, the sooner you can be about that business and be effectively competent.

I think men, especially, make one of two very common mistakes. One is that some of us think we can do everything. As time goes by, we eventually realize this is not true and that it is not in God's design or economy for us. On the other end, which is equally as bad, we think we can't do anything.

Christians often falsely believe that's being humble. I think it's an insult to God for any of His children to say, "I can't do anything. I'm just kind of normal and average." That's not humility, it's an affront to the God who created and invested in us.

You can be everything God wants you to be.

For it is God who is at work in you, enabling you both to will and to work for his good pleasure.
(Philippians 2:13)

God has been working in us all along since before we even arrived on earth. Then the moment we got introduced to and said "yes" to Christ,

God came to take up residence in us to help us to identify and fulfill the assignment that He has given us. However, to carry out our assignment, we need resources. There are basically two key components. One involves the abilities, talents, and the capacity to do something exceptionally well by using them. Then on the other side is the interest, passion, and the emotional element of enjoying and loving to do something exceptionally well.

I think that's what He's describing when he says, "God is at work in you both to will and to work for His good pleasure." To will is to create the desire, the passion, and the interest in our lives. Then to work is to produce the talents, the gifts, and the capacity to do it exceptionally well.

There are two ways to discover our God-given abilities. One is what I call an "Aha moment." These people have known from the time they were eight-twelve years of age what they were going to be the rest of their lives. There are a few of those, but I can tell you they're not the norm; they're the exception. For most of us, it is a process—sometimes a lifelong process.

Our abilities are a blending of three major contributors. The first one is our natural talent. These are those things that were largely innate and we were born with them. Just watch your children or grandchildren for the first two or three years of life. I have a grandchild going on six years of age, and I'm already seeing what this grandchild can be good at. I can see it very well in my fourteen-year-old grandson, and my twelve-year-old granddaughter. As parents and grandparents, we need to help these children develop these natural talents.

Added to those innate talents, we also have potential strengths. Strengths are developed out of our basic talents, but strengths are not just what we're good at. Strengths are the things that we do that make us feel strong. We're in our strength zone when we're doing something and time just flies by.

Then when we come to Christ, we get these Spiritual Gifts that I think augment and amplify that which God uniquely put in us at birth so we can be really exceptional if not excellent at those things. Identifying our abilities is critical.

The second area is passions. Passions are the desires that are innately put in us by God for certain people, topics, and activities that give us focus and energy. Passionless areas bore us, drain us, and suck the life out of us. You will know something is a strength for you when you really look forward to doing it. Then when you're doing it, you're in the zone. Then when you finish doing it, you go "yes." Passion gives you energy and purpose in life.

Identifying Abilities and Passions

Number One: Clearly identify your best abilities and wisely allocate those resources.

Number Two: Gain all the knowledge you can in all the ways you can to learn more about your top abilities and passions. Read about them and talk to others that you think are good at some of the same things you're good at. Observe and pay attention, and don't just be robotic. Don't just go through the motions.

Number Three: Select specific skills to work on and to improve that will enhance your best abilities.

Number Four: Deliberately practice using your top talents in order to gain valuable experience. I think it was Malcolm Gladwell Outliers that said it takes about ten years or 10,000 hours to become an expert at something. The factor that seems to explain the most about great performance is something that researchers call deliberate practice. Find out what you're really good at and deliberately and intentionally get better at it.

Number Five: Discover when and where you are the most productive. Are you most productive in morning, during the afternoon or at night? Is it in a busy place, a quiet place, cluttered place, or a neat place? Do you know what activities and people energize you and which ones drain you? You've got to have self-awareness to be exceptionally competent.

Number Six: Discipline yourself to stay focused, to work hard, and to build strong habits. Discipline is tough, but worth it.

Number Seven: Leverage your greatness to your advantage for greater influence. What you're exceptionally good at is your competitive advantage. It's what makes you stand out.

Number Eight: Share the knowledge of your best abilities with family, boss, and colleagues. They can help you improve and build on them.

Number Nine: Develop a strategy to align your top abilities with your job.

Number Ten: Keep growing and developing in your abilities by practicing and being deliberate.

Benefits of Exceptional Competence

Number One: It increases your engagement and helps you become emotionally energized at what you do. Gallup research says that when a person is able to spend most of their day doing what they do best and enjoy most, they're six times more engaged in their work.

Number Two: It increases your fulfillment. When you're doing what you enjoy most and do best, it gives you meaning and purpose and your well-being triples.

Number Three: It increases your productivity. If you're doing what you do best and enjoy most, your productivity goes up, you feel better, and you perform better.

Number Four: It increases your opportunity. You get better at what you do and that often brings more opportunity for advancement.

A Word of Warning

Remember that character trumps talent.

Be careful as you develop exceptional competency and make sure your character development keeps up with it. Read the stories of the Enron fall. Read the stories of all of those CEO's who fell because of character issues. When they started they were men of character, but as their competencies went up and their opportunities went up and their pay went up and their entitlement went up, their character didn't keep up and that was the problem.

In Proverbs 22:29 it says, "Do you see a man skillful in his work? He will stand before kings; he will not stand before obscure men." That Hebrew verb *stand* means to serve, stand up, take a position, present oneself, and to have greater influence. As you get better at who you are and what you do, God's going to give you a larger platform to make a difference.

Find Your Sweet Spot

Do things that you enjoy, then love doing them exceptionally well.

Your abilities plus your passions equal your sweet spot. I grew up playing primarily three sports: basketball, golf, and baseball. In golf and baseball, when you hit that certain spot on the ball, it just launches and off it goes. Its sweet spot. You and I have a sweet spot and the sooner we find it the better.

If you can find a career where you get to do what you enjoy and what you're really good at, and to top it all off, they pay you to do it, that's your sweet spot. It provides focus, energy, and passion and it's not a job anymore. It's not a career anymore. It's who you are and you get paid to do it. Every man and woman ought to be looking for their sweet spot.

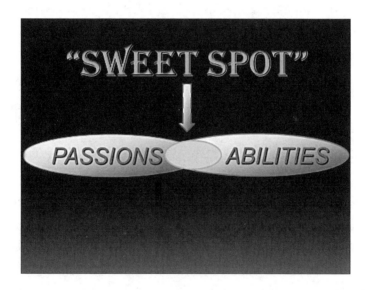

QUESTIONS FOR SELF-REFLECTION
CHAPTER FOUR—COMPETENCY

1. *Who are some exceptionally competent people that inspire you and why?*

2. *How does greater competency open the door for greater influence?*

3. *What did you learn from Jimmy's teaching on Psalm 139:13-16?*

4. *Can you name your greatest abilities and deepest passions?*

5. *Why will developing your strengths, rather than improving your weaknesses, give you greater competence?*

6. *What was your best learning from this chapter and how can you apply it today?*

7. *What percentage of your work allows you to do what you do best and enjoy most?*

8. *Which of Jimmy's ten suggestions most challenge you?*

9. *What are some specific actions you could take to increase your knowledge, skills, and abilities to increase your overall competency?*

10. *Is Proverbs 22:29 proving true in your life?*

Chapter 5

The Connections of a Leader Worth Following

Relationships largely define who we are and what we become. Go all the way back to the beginning in creation when God made Adam and then He made Eve because it was not good for man to be alone. Then came the family and then society, so from the beginning God's plan had a lot to do with relationships. In fact, there's really no way to be an effective leader much less one worth following if you're not willing to invest in building meaningful, personal relationships. When Jesus was asked, "What's the greatest commandment?" His answer was to love God and love others. It's all about building meaningful relationships.

I've seen men and women of great character who ended up needing to be let go from a company because they were a thorn in every human relationship. It is inexcusable for us not to be leaders who are seeking to build relationships and forgive even the most difficult people no matter what because every one of us have been on the other end of that forgiveness. There's not anything anybody would ever do to us that we've not done or thought about doing, yet God has forgiven us. Not to forgive someone and not to forgive yourself is to elevate yourself above God and you don't want to go there. Psalm 78:72 says, "David shepherded them with integrity of heart and with skillful hands he led them." Shepherds care for, protect, lead, guide, nurture, and know their sheep. Regardless of the size of the flock, a shepherd could look at his sea of white lambs and know every one of them and know when one was lost. Every one of them was personal to the shepherd.

What you and I need to realize is that our lives are full of sheep. We're married to one. Our kids are sheep. The people we work with are sheep. Like the shepherd's sheep, at times they can be cantankerous and they can stink, but the shepherd never discarded them. You and I don't have the privilege of discarding them either. Our role is to do whatever is needed by the sheep at any given moment in the relationship. That means we've got to be sensitive and flexible as well.

When we deepen the relationships with the sheep, it increases the influence and the results as well. In Mark 3:14, Jesus appointed twelve disciples so that they might be with Him and preach with Him. The relational aspect came prior to the assignment.

Where we get in trouble, both at home and with other relationships, is when the rules and regulations begin to take precedence over the relationship. One of our sons had an issue with a friend and we were chatting about it.

He said, "You know, Daddy, I'm not sure what to do. The guy's really been a good friend for a long time."

I said, "Don't lose the relationship. Whatever you guys are in disagreement over is not worth losing the relationship. Even if you think he's more wrong than you are, swallow your pride, seek forgiveness and restore, rebuild, and strengthen the relationship. That will take humility and brokenness, especially when you don't feel you're the one at fault, but do it. The relationship is more important than anything else. This guy's been a good influence and a good friend in your life for a long time. Don't walk away. It's not worth it."

Building a Meaningful Relationship

What does it take to connect with people and build a meaningful relationship? Granted, some people are innately gifted with great people skills. However, I do think it's something that all of us can get better at. I came across these statements that were put on a job application by folks that were looking for work. They had lost their previous jobs and this is what they put down on their applications as to why.

- *It's best for employers if I don't work with people.*
- *The company made me a scapegoat just like my previous employers.*
- *Please don't misconstrue my fourteen jobs as job-hopping. I've never quit a job.*
- *I have no references. I've left a path of destruction everywhere I went.*

I think one thing that has negatively impacted our ability to build meaningful relationships is social media. Texting, instant messaging, tweeting, and Facebook have given us great ways to stay connected to people, yet never has our society been more relationally disconnected.

We may have more relationships, more acquaintances, more casual friends, but we're having fewer deep connections and fewer deep relationships because we can keep them at bay through technology. How many contacts do you have in your phone? These are folks you have immediate access to, but how many of them could you call at 2 a.m. in the morning?

Steve Saccone's book, "Relational Intelligence," and Marshall Goldsmith's great book entitled, "What Got You Here Won't Get You

There," are books that talk about the costliest, relational sins and where we do most damage in our relationships. Sometimes we know and sometimes we're unaware of what we're doing. Here is a combination of the things that damage relationships that I pulled from these two books.

- *Don't assume your way is always best. It usually means it's not.*
- *Don't give unsolicited advice. People prefer to trust you first; they're funny that way.*
- *See how long you can go without promoting yourself. It's harder than you think.*
- *Don't state the obvious just because you don't have anything profound to say. Sometimes silence is golden.*
- *Don't be bossy. Remember in kindergarten when they taught you that no one likes a know it all.*
- *Stop avoiding conflict, but don't create it either.*
- *Don't self-deprecate for appearance's sake. That's what your spouse is for.*
- *Don't talk more than what you are willing to do. Actions speak louder than words.*
- *Fight the temptation to "one up" someone with a better story than theirs. It's hard to believe, but sometimes people have better stories than you do.*
- *Don't appear more engaged than you are. We know when you're faking it.*

You can deal with people in one of two ways. You can be relational or you can be what I call transactional. Men tend to be transactional. By transactional I mean we tend to build a lot of our relationships based on deals because the world in which we work is driven by deals. It's driven by transactions. If you do that seven to twelve hours a day four to six days a week, it develops a mentality that every relationship you have, even with your spouse and kids, becomes transactional. In other words, I'll do something for you if you'll do something for me. That does not build long term, lasting, meaningful personal relationships. Being relational does.

A question was asked, "Why is it hard to find good male leaders?" The answers were, it's because we train men for work and not for relationships. Number two, males tend to avoid involvement when they believe that they might fail. Males are often emotionally impaired. Our culture has a faulty image of true masculinity. Males tend to carry a wrong view of what leadership is and what it does. However, there are ways to build meaningful relationships that we can all put into practice whether at home or at work.

Building Meaningful Relationships

Number One: Be comfortable with who you are. If you're not comfortable with you, you're not going to be able to make meaningful relationships with anybody else because they're not going to be comfortable with you either. You've got to get comfortable in your own skin. That's why we talked about character, dealing with flaws, fixing you, and developing your walk with God. How you and I see ourselves is going to have a tremendous impact on how we perceive and see others.

Number Two: Unconditionally love those that you are privileged to influence. Care more about the relationship than the rules. Charles Swindoll is one of my favorite writers, and he called it the ABC's of love.

A - I **accept** you as a person.

B - I **believe** that you have value.

C - I **care** for you especially when you hurt.

D - I **desire** the very best for you.

E - I **erase** all of your sins against me.

Number Three: Look for every opportunity to use your influence for their good. It's more about what we give than what we get. We ought to be asking ourselves, "How can I help you? How can I help you succeed? How can I add value to your life?" We have a tendency, to over-promise and under-deliver in our relationships. We're better off reversing that and look for every opportunity to add value to others so the focus is off us.

Number Four: Remain accessible, approachable, and accountable. People want you to answer three questions for them. "Can I trust you? Do you really care about me? Are you for me, against me, or for yourself?" It is really all about motive.

Number Five: Remain authentic and transparent with others. A lot of this has to do with communication. Relationships often get impaired because we aren't authentic and transparent in our communication with others. We get frustrated because people don't meet our expectations when the problem is we never told them about these expectations in the first place. We assumed they would figure it out. We felt they ought to know what pleases us, what frustrates us, and what angers us, though most of us have never communicated that to those that we spend most of our time with. We need to let people know by being authentic and transparent.

Number Six: Lead people gently. Do not control them. I have to watch this because I can be a very controlling person. You know you are a controlling person when:

- *People start apologizing prior to approaching you because they're afraid you're going to react.*
- *You assume they all approve of you.*
- *You assume you are always right.*
- *You like to hold onto knowledge because it gives you control.*
- *You think you ought to be involved in making all of the decisions.*
- *You think that you ought to have the final word in every decision.*
- *You're afraid of others being in control of another project.*

Number Seven: Strive to be a good and active listener. Show people you care by really listening. The two words are anagrams, listen and silent because they use the same letters just arranged in a different order. James 1:19 says, "Be slow to speak and quick to listen." Maybe that's why God gave us two ears and one mouth.

Number Eight: Strive not to overreact to the small stuff. Some of us are just overly sensitive. Everything somebody says or does bothers us. Don't disrupt a relationship over something that's really nothing just because you have got to win. If you've got to win every battle, you're probably going to lose the relationship. Aggressively forgive and aggressively extend grace because in all likelihood you're going to need to be on the other end of it someday. Pick your battles wisely.

Number Nine: Recognize and reward those who get things done the right way whether it's a spouse, a child, a co-worker, somebody that works for you, or somebody you work for. We live in a hurting world. I don't know that I've ever had anybody over-appreciate me and you probably haven't either. We live in a world surrounded by people that hardly ever hear any words of affirmation or appreciation much less reward or recognition. Look for every opportunity to say they have done a good job.

I wish I had always used this method while coaching, but I have told my son in regard to our grandson who is playing basketball, use the 3/1 rule. When you're on the way home after a game, tell him three things that he did well, then tell him the one thing he needs to work on. When I coached I think I had the 1/9 rule. I would tell them one good thing and then nine things they needed to work on. Affirmation goes a long, long way in building relationships.

Number Ten: Cultivate deeper relationships with a few, vital friends. Casual friends are the outer circle of acquaintances. Vital friends are the inner circle. We all need them. Write down your top five closest relationships outside of family and then next to that write down what you contribute to each relationship and what they contribute to the relationship.

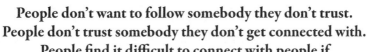

**People don't want to follow somebody they don't trust.
People don't trust somebody they don't get connected with.
People find it difficult to connect with people if
they don't know our heart.**

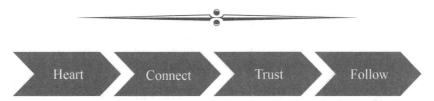

We want to influence people. We want people to follow us. We want people to let us speak into their lives. We want to have full impact on people. To do that, they have to believe we're credible. They have to connect with us. We've got to show ourselves to them by being transparent.

We've got to be willing to be transparent and vulnerable and that's hard for guys.

C.S. Lewis said there is no "safe investment." To paraphrase his thoughts: *To love at all is to be vulnerable. Loving anything and your heart will certainly be wrung and possibly be broken. If you want to make sure of keeping it intact, you must give your heart to no one; not even to an animal. Wrap it carefully around with hobbies and little luxuries, avoid all entanglements, lock it up safe in the casket or coffin of your own selfishness. But in that casket, safe, dark, motionless and airless, your heart will change. It will not be broken. I will become unbreakable and impenetrable. The alternative to tragedy or at least to the risk of tragedy is damnation. The only place outside heaven where you can be perfectly safe from all dangers of love is hell. Take the risk.*

As Christians and aspiring influencers and leaders, if we can't establish and maintain meaningful connections then our effectiveness is going to be minimized. Though character and competency are important, don't underestimate the importance of this relational connection. Your legacy is what people will remember about you and me. So, we need to make sure we live every day the way that we want to be remembered. We won't get another shot.

> *Love is patient and kind; love does not envy or boast; it is not arrogant or rude. It does not insist on its own way; it is not irritable or resentful; it does not rejoice at wrongdoing, but rejoices with the truth. Love bears all things, believes all things, hopes all things, endures all things.*
>
> (1 Corinthians 13:4-7)

In these four verses, Paul is describing what real, true, biblical, sacrificial, self-less love looks like which is fundamental for building relationships. There are fifteen different qualities or characteristics of love within

74

this passage. Eight of them are negative. Seven of them are positive. I want you to read through the passage and think about which two you need to work on today.

The stronger the relationship, the higher the relational equity, the greater the capacity to have an impact on somebody else's life.

QUESTIONS FOR SELF-REFLECTION
CHAPTER FIVE—CONNECTIONS

1. *What is your response to Jimmy's statement: Relationships define who we are and what we become?*
2. *According to Jimmy's definition of a leader based on Mark 3:14, do you agree that leadership is both directional and relational?*
3. *If you improved your relationships, do you think it could enhance your influence?*
4. *How has social media and technology impacted our ability to build meaningful relationships and connections?*
5. *Which of Steve Saccone's "Top Ten Relational Sins" are most true in your life?*
6. *If you honestly examined your closest relationships, are they built more on transactions than meaningful connections?*
7. *What was your best learning from this chapter and how can you apply it today?*
8. *Jimmy offered ten tips for building better connections. Which ones need your attention?*
9. *How do you feel about Jimmy's sequence for building better relational connections?*

Chapter 6

Servant Leadership

As Christians, we can't discuss leadership without looking at the life of Jesus and how He described leadership. Think about how you would answer each of the following questions. If you really want a balanced outlook on this, ask someone you respect to answer these questions about you as well.

1. *Do I tend to serve more out of obligation or joyful obedience?*
2. *Do I tend to care more about what others see or what God sees?*
3. *Is my attitude more often "it is not my job" or "whatever it takes"?*
4. *Is my agenda more "me first" or "others first"?*
5. *Do I have more of a spirit of pride or humility?*
6. *Are my results more self-seeking or God-glorifying?*
7. *Do I tend to be more annoyed or honored if someone asks me to serve?*

What Christian Leadership Should Look Like

In Mark 10:35-45, Jesus had a discussion with His disciples about what Christian leadership should look like. It starts out with two of His disciples approaching Him with a question that probably amazed most of us the first time we read it.

And James and John, the sons of Zebedee, came up to Him and said to Him, "Teacher, we want you to do for us whatever we ask."

They were saying, we don't want to tell you yet what we want, we just want to get your commitment that you're going to do what we ask. However, Jesus answered them by asking a question we would probably all love for God to ask us. These two disciples were probably very pleased at His response as well.

And He said to them, "What do you want me to do?" And they said, "Grant us to sit, one at your right hand and one at the left, in your glory."

They had figured out from His teaching that Jesus was setting up a new kind of kingdom. They were basically asking that when He came into His kingdom and set up His throne, if they could occupy the thrones on either side of Him. Perhaps they felt the hours of overtime they had put in and the tasks He had asked them to do had somehow qualified them for these positions. However, Jesus basically responds by telling them they are clueless to what would be required to be appointed to such leadership positions.

Jesus said to them, "You do not know what you're asking. Are you able to drink the cup that I drink, or to be baptized with the baptism with which I am baptized?" And they said to Him, "We are able." And Jesus said to them, "The cup that I drink you will drink, and with the baptism with which I am baptized, you will be baptized, but to sit at my right hand or my left is not mine to grant, but it is for those for whom it has been prepared." And when the ten heard this, they began to be indignant at James and John.

Here we have a management nightmare. Two of His trainees now think they outrank their co-workers for some reason and have ticked these other guys off.

And Jesus called them to Him and said to them. "You know that those who are considered rulers, leaders of the Gentiles lord it over them, and their great ones exercise authority over them. But [here's a contrast] it shall not be so among you." [Not those who follow me. Not those who know me.] "But whoever would be great among you must be your servant, and whoever would be first among you must be slave of all. For even the Son of Man came not to be served but to serve, and to give [to invest] His life as a ransom for many."

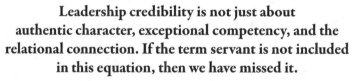

Leadership credibility is not just about authentic character, exceptional competency, and the relational connection. If the term servant is not included in this equation, then we have missed it.

Jesus defined leadership in general in Mark 3:14 when He called those twelve to be with Him and then sent them out on a mission. In Mark 10:35-45, Matthew 20, and Luke 22, He's describing what this credible Christian leader looks and acts like. Servanthood is what Jesus is describing in these passages.

A working definition of a servant leader is someone who willingly—not begrudgingly, not annoyingly, but humbly and sacrificially serves others. Serving others always costs us in time and energy. There's no way to serve and not pay the piper. Willingly, humbly, sacrificially, intentionally, and deliberately choosing to serve defines a servant leader. It means not waiting for anyone to ask for help. Servant leadership means looking for ways to serve even before we are asked.

Jesus modeled servant leadership. Jesus is with those that have followed Him so closely the last three years in an upper room. He's got an intense agenda facing Him that His disciples have no clue is going to start in just a few hours.

Now before the Feast of the Passover, when Jesus saw that His hour had come to depart out of this world to the Father, having loved His own who were in the world, He loved them to the end. During supper, when the devil had already put it into the heart of Judas Iscariot, Simon's son, to betray Him, Jesus, knowing that the Father had given all things into His hands, and that He had come from God and was going back to God, rose from supper. He laid aside His outer garments, taking a towel, tied it around His waist. Then He poured water into a basin and began to wash the disciples' feet and to wipe them with the towel that was wrapped around Him. He came to Simon Peter, who said to Him, "Lord, do You wash my feet." Jesus answered him, "What I am doing you do not understand now, but afterward you will understand." Peter said to Him, "You'll never wash my feet." Jesus answered, "If I don't wash you then you have no share with Me." Simon Peter said to Him, [then give me a bath- that's in the Knott standard version there] Jesus said to him, "The one who has bathed does not need to wash except for his feet, but is completely clean. And you are clean, but not every one of you. For he who was to betray Him; that was why He said, "Not all of you are clean." When He had washed their feet and put on His outer garments and resumed His place, He said to them, "Do you understand what I have done to you? You call me Teacher and Lord, and you are right, for so I am. If I then, your Lord and Teacher, have washed your feet, you also ought to wash one another's feet. For I have given you an example, that you should also do just as I have done to you. Truly, truly I say to you, a servant is not greater than his master, nor is a messenger greater than the one who sent him. If you know these things, blessed are you if you do them." (John 13:1-17)

Servant leaders put others first. That's what He's talking about in the opening verses.

He said having loved His own, He loved them to the end. It's selflessness even though He had an intense agenda coming up. Jesus is showing us that even when our agenda is overloaded, it's others first.

Servant leaders have a loving heart. No one has to serve, but for those of us who know Christ, we ought to serve because we love others because Christ loved us. He served us to the end because of His great love for us.

Servant leaders are secure in who they are. "Jesus, knowing that the Father had given all things into His hands, and that He had come from God and was going back to God" (John 13:3).

Jesus knew who He was, where He had come from, why He was here, and where He was going.

Jesus was comfortable in all of those. Folks that aren't comfortable in their own skin will rarely serve others for the right reasons. Insecure people do not make good servants because it's all about self-preservation and self-promotion. We've got to be comfortable in our own skin or we will spend more time defending ourselves and protecting ourselves than giving ourselves away.

Barna research found that less than 10 percent of evangelical Christians know what the Bible says and seek to live out the scriptural answers to: Who am I? Where did I come from? What is my purpose? What is my destiny? Those are the fundamental questions of life that Jesus was comfortable in answering.

Servant leaders serve everyone. "During supper, when the devil had already put into the heart of Judas Iscariot, Simon's son, to betray Him." Jesus knew this and still washed the man's feet.

Servant leaders don't keep score. Think of someone you don't really care for. You love them in Jesus' name, but would you wash their feet? A few years ago a couple showed up here at the church and I had the joy of leading them to Christ. Then he just kind of latched onto me; from my perspective, annoyingly so. Sunday and Wednesday he was like a shadow, asking me, "Can we do this? Can we do that?" One day, I said, "Joe, I've got a life to live here, back off." God really began to work in his life. He began to grow and he felt a calling to a vocational ministry. He and his wife were loading up to head off to seminary.

He caught me on his last Sunday here and he said, "Hey, are you in this week?" I couldn't think of a way out of it, so I finally told him to call my assistant and we'll schedule it. He came by my office that week, sat down across the desk from me holding a briefcase. We exchanged some pleasantries for a few moments and then he said, "Hey, would you come around and sit by me?" He moved to the other chair and I sat down next to him.

He took his briefcase, set it in his lap and pulled out a kind of sandwich bag. He reached in and pulled out a wet washcloth. He then asked if he could take off my shoes and socks, and proceeded to put first one foot then the other in his hand, took that wet washcloth, and he washed my feet. Then he took a towel that he brought with him and he dried them. He put my socks and shoes back on, put everything back in the briefcase, closed it up, gave me a bear hug, and walked out.

I've never forgotten how I felt after that experience. He went on and finished seminary and ended up the President of a Bible College in North Carolina. Later on, he developed a brain tumor and died and I never saw him again. But I never forgot Joe, and I never will. You remember true servants. I share that story every chance that I get to keep Joe's memory alive and to encourage you and me to live more like Joe and to be a servant leader.

Servant leaders are not position conscience. You know it's interesting that the disciples wanted to label Jesus. They called Him Teacher and Lord. However, Jesus reversed that and said you call me Lord and Teacher and you are right. Jesus was not hung up on titles or positions and neither should we. You don't have to have a title to be a leader. You don't have to have a title to serve other people. You've just got to be deliberate and hopefully do it for the right reason.

True servant leaders initiate, they act. This guy called me and invited me to lunch. About halfway through lunch, he started unloading on his wife saying how she's not this, she's not that, she doesn't do this, and she doesn't do that. I just kind of let him ramble and finished my meal. Then I said, "Are you done throwing your wife under the bus? If you are then I've got one question for you. What are you doing to serve your wife? When was the last time you looked your wife in the face and said, 'How can I serve you?' Thank you for lunch. Don't call me again until you've been able to successfully answer that question."

If you're not willingly serving the one that God put you in a permanent relationship with on this planet and that you've purported to love, honor, and cherish until death do you part, then you don't get it. You will never really be the head of the household much less the Christian leader that you need to be if it doesn't start at home.

Are You a Servant Leader?

Think of someone you consider to be a servant leader. I'll bet you some, if not all of these attributes Jesus listed are true in their life. That's what made them a servant leader in your eyes. Does anyone think of you as a servant leader?

When was the last time you asked someone how you could help them or serve them or make life better for them?

What would be on your résumé, if you could only include the accomplishments others say you enabled them to attain because you served them? You can't put education or work experience or skills learned or strengths on it. How long would your résumé be?

If your influence as a leader was solely based on your service to others, how impactful would you be?

How do You Attain Greatness?

A dispute also arose among them, as to which of them was to be regarded as the greatest. And He said to them, "The kings of the Gentiles exercise lordship over them, and those in authority over them are called benefactors. But not so with you. Rather, let the greatest among you be as the youngest, and the leader as the one who serves. For who is the greater, one who reclines at the table or one who serves? Is it not the one who reclines at the table? But I am among you as the one who serves."

(Luke 22:24-27)

Servant Leadership equals greatness. Don't you find it interesting that when they approached Jesus arguing among themselves as to who would be the greatest that Jesus did not even address their aspiration? He did not reprimand them for having ambition, wanting to be successful, and wanting to be great. What He did was clarify how to attain greatness. It is through service. It's okay to have aspirations driven by the Holy Spirit. Success with the right definition can potentially position you and me for greater opportunity for influence. There's nothing wrong with that. However, His disciples were arguing over who was going to sit where on the thrones and Jesus' answer was, "It's not about where you sit on a throne, it's about picking up a towel."

We don't do that for the reward either. One of the rewards we do receive, though, is we become more like Jesus. I love what Pastor David said, "We're never more like Jesus than when we're serving." Do you want to become more like Jesus? Be a servant leader. Another reward is that we will be blessed as a result of serving others in this way. He says I will bless those whose heart is to serve others.

This kind of leadership goes against our nature. It certainly goes against the culture in which we live. It is not easy. That's why it has to be willingly, humbly, sacrificially, and intentionally done.

Leadership is not about title, position or personality. It is about making other's lives better by serving them.

QUESTIONS FOR SELF-REFLECTION
CHAPTER SIX—SERVANT LEADERSHIP

1. *What are the differences between a servant leader and a self-serving leader?*

2. *Outside the Bible, who are some servant leaders who influenced you and how so?*

3. *Jimmy defined a servant leader as someone who willingly, humbly, sacrificially, and intentionally serves others. Is anything missing from his definition?*

4. *How do you respond to Jimmy's assertion, "Serving defines both the why (our motivation) and the how (methodology) we should have"?*

5. *In John 13, Jesus models servant leadership by washing the disciple's feet. Jimmy identified five marks of a servant leader: others first (vv. 1-5), loving heart (v. 1), secure self (v. 3), impartially serves everyone (vv. 2, 10, 11), and takes action (vv. 13-17). How do you feel about these and are there others he did not mention? Which mark do you need to improve?*

6. *Earlier we asked you to think of a life example of servanthood. What are the chances someone thought this of you?*

7. *If those who know you best were asked to describe you, would they include "servant?"*

8. When was the last time you asked someone, "How could I help (serve) you?"

9. What would be on your resume if you could only include the accomplishments others say you enabled them to attain because you served them?

10. If you were paid $10 only when you served others, how well would you do?

11. How do you feel about Jimmy's comment, "We are never more like Jesus than when we are serving"?

12. What was your best learning from this chapter and how can you apply it today?

Chapter 7

Your Toughest Leadership Challenge

"If there were to be a sudden change in cabin pressure, the mask drops down. Put on your own mask first and then take care of any children with you."

Thousands and thousands of times all over the globe that speech is given. At first that really sounds very selfish, yet if you're not breathing yourself, you can't help the child breathe. If you don't take care of you, you can't take care of others. If you can't lead yourself, you're not going to be able to lead others. You and I have got to pay close attention to our own oxygen mask.

If you can't lead you, why should anyone else let you influence them? If they're watching your life and see areas that are out of control and you try to speak into their lives, why should they listen to you? Self-leadership is kind of the entrance exam to leading others. If you don't pass that test, then you're probably not going to have influence on those around you. Self-leadership is really what leads to a credible, successful leadership in life.

In 1 Samuel 30:1-3, David was a king in the making. He'd been in the battle with King Saul and he'd had great success. God was really blessing the military campaigns under his leadership and he was winning battle after battle.

Then it says, "Now when David and his men came to Ziklag on the third day, the Amalekites had made a raid against the Negeb and against Ziklag. They had overcome Ziklag and burned it with fire and taken captive the women and all who were in it, both small and great. They killed no one, but carried them off and went their way. When David and his men came to the city, they found it burned with fire, and their wives and sons and daughters taken captive."

When they came back home after being on the battlefield, everything they had was burned and the people they loved the most were gone. "Then David and the people who were with him raised their voices and wept until they had no more strength to weep. David's two wives also had been taken captive. And David was greatly distressed. For the people spoke of stoning him."

If you're in David's situation what's your next move? Do you speak to the captains and rally the troops? Notice what David did. "But David strengthened himself." He prepared himself, he got a hold of himself, he gripped himself, "in the Lord his God." You've got to have God's help to be a good leader.

One of the first things we need to consider in taking care of ourselves first is to go before the Lord and ask Him to give us the guidance and the strength we need to lead the people He has called us to lead. When they see us turning to God first, it will instill confidence in them as well.

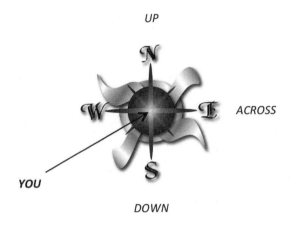

UP

ACROSS

YOU

DOWN

What Is Self-Leadership?

Aristotle said the hardest victory is over self. Daniel Goleman's book, *Emotional Intelligence*, is basically about self-understanding and self-awareness. Dee Hock, the Founder and CEO of VISA, has spent his retirement years developing a leadership think tank to train, develop, and to grow men and women in leadership. There are basically four areas of influence we have as a leader. There are those we are in direct leadership over, there are those who pass through our lives and we have an opportunity to influence, and there are those in authority over us. Yes, we are often called to influence those over us as well as those under us. However, Hock's research shows we only need to spend about 5 percent of our time touching the people below us, about 20 percent with our peers, 25 percent influencing those in authority over us, and 50 percent on self-leadership development. Most leaders are surprised at this until they realize the principle of the oxygen mask.

Self-leadership development is necessary in order to effectively lead others whether they are under us, over us or our peers. It is important that we understand what self-leadership is and how we go about developing it. Self-leadership is the awareness of and the ability to manage our own strengths, weaknesses, limitations, emotions, and temptations. It's the ability to influence ourselves and how we think, feel, and act so we can achieve what we want out of life.

In other words, the first question you must ask is, *"What does success look like to you?"* You get up every morning chasing it whether intentionally or subconsciously. However, an even more important question is whether that ladder you're climbing toward your goal is leaning against the wall that God wants it leaning against. If it isn't, your level of success is going to be severely limited.

Bill Hybels says in his book, *Courageous Leadership*, we need to take whatever steps we need to in order to become proficient by taking care of what's going on in our life first. Bill George, who teaches in the Harvard Business School, talks about understanding our "True North," which he defines as our core values, our purpose, and where we are heading in life. He wrote an article some time ago in the Harvard Business Review, "Discovering Your Authentic Leadership." In it are the results of the largest in-depth study ever taken on how authentic leadership fuels effectiveness and success. The article describes a critical component that every leader needs in his or her journey toward authentic leadership. In one study when seventy-five members of the Stanford Graduate School of Business Advisory Council were asked to recommend the most important capability for leaders to develop, their answer was nearly unanimous and agreed with Bill George—self-awareness.

If we want to gain an accurate view of ourselves, we must consistently invest in our internal growth potential not just in external success. To do this, we need to know what God's purpose for us is and what abilities He has placed within us to achieve that purpose. When we find the courage to look inside without allowing the filters of self-protection and self-preservation to blind us, it opens up a vista to personal growth that we never even knew was possible.

Tim Irwin, in "Run with the Bulls," has a section called self-management. He says the ability to manage ourselves and to manage our relationships is heavily dependent on a perceptiveness of what's going on within us and with others. Self and other awareness employs the ability to discern our own thoughts and feelings as well as the thoughts and feelings of others. Those who derail on their journey to fulfilling their purpose seem to lack that ability to discern. It sets us up for failure.

Why? If we lack a sense of self-awareness about our strengths, weaknesses, vulnerability, we will also lack the skills we need to relate well to others. Pride, fear, anger, greed, defensiveness, aloofness, suspicion, impatience, and negativity are all warning signs that we often just ignore, but that can stand in the way of effective leadership.

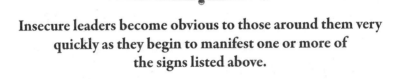

Insecure leaders become obvious to those around them very quickly as they begin to manifest one or more of the signs listed above.

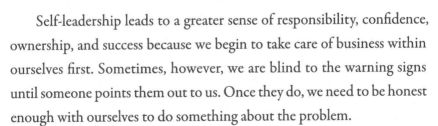

Self-leadership leads to a greater sense of responsibility, confidence, ownership, and success because we begin to take care of business within ourselves first. Sometimes, however, we are blind to the warning signs until someone points them out to us. Once they do, we need to be honest enough with ourselves to do something about the problem.

My dad was a good golfer. He got me started early and by the time I was fifteen, my handicap was zero. I played golf all the way through college. It was so much a part of my life that I planned to go pro, but around the time I was thinking along those lines, my game began to unravel. I didn't have any idea why. After some weeks of really playing poorly, I ran into Tim, a guy I had played a lot of golf with in the past. His daddy was the only optometrist in my small town. When I told him what was happening, he suggested it could be my vision. Though I protested, he suggested I make an appointment with his dad and go see. I finally took his advice. I was totally unaware that my vision was the problem in my game. There was no way for me to experience success because I couldn't see. Somebody had to help me by pointing out the symptom that was obvious to them but not to me.

The Bible speaks often of self-mastery and self-management. Stop for a moment and review these scriptures to discern what God is saying about this important aspect of leadership.

> *Proverbs 29:11 says, "A fool gives full vent to his spirit, but a wise man quietly holds it back."*

> *Proverbs 25:28 adds, "A man without self-control is like a city broken into and left without walls."*

> *Matthew 7:3-5 exhorts us to, "Why do you see the speck that is in your brother's eye, but do not notice the log that is in your own eye? Or how can you say to your brother, 'Let me take the speck out of your eye,' when there is the log in your own eye? You hypocrite, first take the log out of your own eye, and then you will see clearly to take the speck out of your brother's eye."*

> *Romans 12:3 warns us, "For by the grace given to me I say to everyone among you not to think of himself more highly than he ought to think,*

but to think with sober judgment, each according to the measure of faith that God has assigned."

1 Corinthians 9:24 says we should run the race to "obtain it."

In 1 Timothy 4:7 Paul says, "Have nothing to do with irreverent, silly myths. Rather train yourself for godliness."

Dealing with Blind Spots

Several years ago, I went through an exercise asking some men in my life to help me identify my blind spots. Now, I thought I knew myself very well, so I told them they could talk to anybody they wanted to, but in thirty days we're going to meet and I wanted them to tell me my blind spots. At the same time, I created my own list of what I perceived as my blind spots.

When we got back together they told me what they thought my blind spots were. I had my list in front of me, but the two they said were my main ones weren't on my list. I missed them completely. I was truly blind to them even though I thought I had it all figured out.

Socrates says, "An unexamined life is not worth living."

Dealing with Failure

This leads to another self-leadership area we must all eventually deal with. The question is not if we will fail, because we all will fail at one time or another in our lives. We will make mistakes. So, how do we regain that credibility as a leader when we fail?

1. *Admit you made a mistake.* Take personal responsibility and don't blame anybody else. Whatever the case may be, it starts with admitting the mistake, the failure, the sin and taking personal responsibility for it. No victim mentality allowed.

2. *Apologize for it.* You can't make them forgive you, but it is your responsibility to admit it and to seek forgiveness. Seek forgiveness from God knowing He, God, will forgive you but it doesn't mean others will.

3. *Accept the consequences whether you deem them fair or not.*

4. *Act to correct it.* If there is restitution needed, do it. Establish a growth plan for those areas that require the greatest attention. Whether it is blind spots, temptation, character flaws or competencies, begin to take action to correct it.

5. *Ask for accountability and accept direction in establishing new behaviors.* Seek and be receptive to feedback from multiple sources. Let two or three people speak into your life.

6. *Advance toward the goal.* Determine to finish strong. It's a choice you will make many times a day every day for the rest of your life.

An old Chinese philosopher said, "Knowing others is intelligence; knowing yourself is true wisdom. Mastering others is strength; mastering yourself is true power."

Self-leadership always leads to exceptional leadership, but you have got to put your own oxygen mask on first.

QUESTIONS FOR-SELF REFLECTION
CHAPTER SEVEN—YOUR TOUGHEST LEADERSHIP CHALLENGE

1. *Jimmy stated, "Your toughest leadership challenge is YOU." Do you agree and how does that make you feel?*
2. *Is it fair to declare, "If you can't lead you, then why should anyone let you lead them?"*
3. *Do you agree that self-leadership precedes successful leadership?*
4. *How do you react to Dee Hock's (Founder of VISA) percentages of what direction we should lead (down-15%, across-15%, up-30% and self-40%)?*
5. *How did the passages from the Bible on self-leadership speak to you?*
6. *What can you add to Jimmy's suggestions on how to develop better self-leadership?*
7. *Where do you need to do a better job at leading yourself?*
8. *What was your best learning from this chapter and how can you apply it today?*

Chapter 8

Exemplary Leadership

Lead by Example

Time to enter the final phase of self-leadership development. We need to be willing to lead by example. Entering into his sixteenth season, Ray Lewis sets the tone for practices and has players come to his home during the week for additional film study. Steve Yzerman is a hockey player who leads his team by example even if he has sore muscles. NBA player, Kevin Garnett, is also a leader by example who challenges his teammates to go one-on-one with him. Angels outfielder, Torii Hunter, is described as a vocal guy who leads by example on the field and off the field.

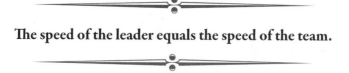

The speed of the leader equals the speed of the team.

People tend to do what they see. People are the picture of the leader. You can't take people where you're not willing to go yourself. It has to do with living the kind of life that people will want, moment by moment, day by day.

When you look at the life of Paul, he basically challenged those who are listening to him to follow his example. Paul certainly didn't say that he had it all together or that he was perfect, but he was a model worth following. Acts 27 contains the narrative. See Appendix 3 for map of Paul's journey to Rome (page 187).

Though Paul hadn't done anything wrong, his presence created such an uproar in the city of Jerusalem that the Roman authorities arrested him. Fearing there was going to be a lynch mob, they transported him at night to Caesarea, eighty miles away from Jerusalem. For the next two years, he appeared before Felix, Festus, the Roman procurators in the area, and then eventually before Herod Agrippa the second. When they found out he was a Roman citizen, they sent him to appear before Nero by ship.

Paul and some other prisoners were handed over to a centurion named Julius who belonged to the imperial regiment. Here is an author paraphrase of what happened on this fateful trip which shows us why Paul can be an example of leadership we can emulate.

To stay out of the Westerly wind and try to manage the ship, they moved along the coast with difficulty and came to a place called Fair Havens, near the town of Lasea. Much time had been lost and sailing had already become dangerous because now it was after the Fast; that's in the fall.

Paul warned them saying, "Men, I can see that our voyage is going to be disastrous and bring great loss to ship and cargo and to our lives also."

But instead of listening to Paul, the centurion follows the advice of the pilot and the owner of the ship. When a gentle wind began to blow, they thought they had obtained what they wanted so they weighed anchor and sailed along the shore of Crete. However, before very long a wind of hurricane force called a northeaster, a typhoon swept down from the island. The ship was caught by the storm and could not head into the wind, so they gave way to it and were driven along heading south.

Blown way off course, they feared they would run aground on the sandbars of the Syrtis off the north shore of Africa, a very dangerous territory. They lowered the sea anchor and let the ship be driven along. It took much violent battering from the storm that next day and they began to throw the cargo overboard to lighten the ship. On the third day they threw the ship's tackle overboard with their own hands. When neither sun nor stars appeared for many days and the storm continued raging, they gave up all hope of being saved.

At this point, Paul stood up before them and said, "Men you should have listened to my advice not to sail from Crete and then you would have spared this damage and loss. But now I urge you to keep up your courage because not one of you will be lost only the ship will be destroyed. Last night, an angel of the God whose I am and whom I serve, stood beside me and said, 'Do not be afraid Paul you must stand trial before Caesar and God has graciously given you the lives of all who sail with you.' So, keep up your courage men for I have faith in God that it will be just as He has told me. Nevertheless, we must run aground on some island." Now they were listening to Paul and he moves to a place of authority in their eyes. He has spoken with confidence that he had a word from God and told them what was going to happen.

Leaders strengthen and build up others.
They think beyond themselves.
They speak into the lives of others and they instill hope.

Once we have walked through difficult times, we begin to realize that when it's all said and done we can put our confidence in God. If we've got God and we've truly put our trust in Him, knowing He makes no mistakes, we can and should be leaders of hope to those around us.

Exemplary leaders live out their convictions.

Remember, earlier Paul said, "Last night an angel of the God whose I am and whom I serve said don't be afraid Paul. You must stand so keep up the courage for I have faith in God that it will happen just as I have told you." Paul shared his convictions and he displayed courage and perseverance.

When the sailors sensed they were approaching land, figuring they would be dashed against the rocks, they dropped four anchors from the stern and prayed for daylight. In an attempt to escape the ship, some of the sailors let the life boat down into the sea pretending that they were going to lower some anchors from the bow.

Paul knew what they were doing and said to the centurion soldiers, "Unless these men stay with the ship they cannot be saved."

Receiving hope and confidence from Paul, the soldiers cut the rope that held the lifeboat and let it fall away. Just before dawn, Paul urged all of them to eat. "Not one of you will lose a single hair upon his head," he told them.

After he said this, he took some bread and gave thanks to God in front of them all and began to eat. They were all encouraged and ate some food themselves.

Paul led by example showing tremendous courage and perseverance. It was not going to be easy, but Paul had the courage and the capacity to say this is what we're going to do and then to lead the way in doing it. He motivated them by setting the example and then got them all involved.

When daylight came they did not recognize the land, but they saw a bay with a sandy beach where they decided to run the ship aground if they could. Cutting loose the anchors they left them in the sea and at the same time untied the ropes that held the rudders. Then they hoisted the foresail to the wind and made for the beach. But the ship struck a sandbar and ran aground. The bow stuck fast and would not move. The stern was broken to pieces by the pounding of the surf. The soldiers planned to kill the prisoners to prevent any of them from swimming away and escaping, but the centurion wanted to spare Paul's life and kept them from carrying out the plan. He ordered those who could swim to jump overboard first to get to land. The rest were to get there on planks. In this way everyone reached land safely.

When they followed the leader God put in their midst, they achieved positive results. Paul was a leader they could follow. He had been through God's training ground, was aware of what God had called him to be and do and then led by example.

Perseverance, encouragement, initiative, competence, determination, discernment, sound judgment, sound decision making, and trustworthiness are the marks of an exemplary leader.

Psalm 78:72 says, "David shepherded them with integrity of heart and with skillful hands he led them." What positioned him to lead and to have influence was that he had character, he was competent, and he was able to connect with others. These characteristics fall under those big "C" words: Character, Competence, and Connection. An exemplary leader is also credible, trustworthy, dependable, reliable, and worth following.

Exemplary leaders take the initiative. We need to be sure that we are more initiators than we are criticizers. It is easy to be critical, negative, and find something not right. However, we need more than the recognition of the problem. We need to be willing to act on the need. Part of establishing credibility is being willing to take the initiative.

Exemplary leaders take the first step. They're willing to step out and they're willing to go first. Several years ago Mel Gibson starred in a movie, "We Were Soldiers." It's the story of the early involvement of the United States in Vietnam. There's a scene in the movie where he's speaking to all of the troops as they're about to move into their first battle. He's addressing the soldiers as they're making their way into this death threatening situation. He said, "I will be the first."

If you watch the movie, his is the first boot on the ground. Toward the end, when they're leaving, the last boot off the ground was also his. We've got to be willing to go first to provide exemplary leadership. I know that's easier for some of us than others, but we've got to do it.

Exemplary leaders exhibit sound judgment and make good decisions. Discernment is needed here. One of the things that tends to cost leaders credibility and get them in trouble personally, martially, and vocationally is making unwise decisions and poor choices. One of the quickest ways to lose a following is to make too many bad decisions.

God's people will tend to be very gracious and forgiving, but at some point you lose the right to lead because you make too many poor decisions. You and I need to be sure that in our decision making several things are in play all the time. We have a choice of attitude and choice of actions on a daily basis. We need to make sure that they're run through the right filter so we minimize the possibility of making damaging decisions and using unsound judgment that not only affects us and our credibility, but could have a negative impact on the other people around us as well.

We need to make sure we're taking care of our own business and our own journey and our own walk first and foremost. To do this we need to be listening to the Holy Spirit and getting the principles we use for decision making from scripture. It's the work of the Holy Spirit wed to the principles of the Word of God where we get the strongest filter to make the wisest decisions.

We also need to get wisdom, advice, and sound counsel from other people. Bring other people into the decision making process; especially people that have added value to our lives in the past. It's not just a matter of getting together for the information. We've got to make sure that the right people are sitting at the table with us to provide the wisdom we need in order to make a wise decision.

Then hopefully, we learn from the bad decisions we may have made and get wiser. Good judgment comes from experience and much of that comes from bad judgment. That's called cowboy wisdom.

Exemplary leaders have God confidence. We can have God confidence if we're willing to listen and act on what God is saying to us. The danger we face is when we put our confidence in our God given ability. We are to use it wisely to help others and to honor and to serve God. That requires time with God in building a relationship with Him through prayer and studying His word. Paul said our sufficiency is of God.

Exemplary leaders strengthen and build up others. They think beyond themselves. They speak into the lives of others, lifting others up, building and strengthening them. There are other focused.

Exemplary leaders instill hope. One of our responsibilities is to try to instill and to foster hope, not just in our own lives, but in the lives of others. Having walked through difficult times, we begin to realize that when it's all said and done if we've got God, family, and a few friends, we're rich. Paul could have been discouraged, depressed, and not said anything to help during the storm, but instead he instilled hope in all those around him. Don't be silent, try to pour life into others through encouraging them.

Exemplary leaders live out their convictions. We all have core values that filter every attitude choice and every decision we make. We're living them every day. We need to make sure they are ones God wants us to have. It's those core values that give us the courage to make the right choices.

Exemplary leaders display courage and perseverance. Paul exhibited tremendous courage and perseverance. He warned us it was not going to be easy, but we need to step up and do what needs to be done whether it's at home or at work.

Exemplary leaders motivate others. To motivate others is to meet their needs. They need to know we care for them. We've got to give them a purpose and a reason to do what we want them to do. Most people also love to be challenged and want to get better at what they're already good at. Tell them they are doing a good job. Recognize, affirm, and pat them on the back. Praise them.

Give them the freedom and the autonomy to manage their time and their energy. Don't stand over them all the time telling them what to do. Invent an enjoyable environment for them to work in.

People also need a role model. They need a picture of how this is supposed to be done. That's our job as a leader and that's what keeps them motivated.

Exemplary leaders get positive results. We would all agree that Jesus was a great leader. Paul was certainly an exemplary leader. I've come to the conclusion that our Lord has never asked us for perfection. All that He has asked out of us as emerging leaders is to be sure we're moving forward in the right direction and growing. As we do, we will see positive results in our relationships with those we are called to lead.

QUESTIONS FOR SELF-REFLECTION
CHAPTER EIGHT—EXEMPLARY LEADERSHIP

1. *Being the right kind of example is one of a leader-worth-following's most powerful tools for influence. Agree or disagree?*

2. *Paul, humbly but boldly challenged people to follow him as he followed Christ. Are you comfortable issuing that same challenge?*

3. *From the narrative of Paul's journey to Rome (Acts 27), Jimmy mentioned ten marks of a leader worth following: credibility, initiative, sound judgment, confidence, strengthens others, instills hope, lives convictions, displays courage and perseverance, and motivates and gets results. Which of these are your strengths and weaknesses? Are there other marks that were overlooked?*

4. *Where can you improve to become more of a leader worth following?*

5. *What was your best learning from our study together?*

DEVELOPING THE SKILLS A LEADER WORTH FOLLOWING MUST POSSESS...

Psalm 78:72

A Psalm of Asaph

And David shepherded them with integrity of heart;
with skillful hands he led them.

Your gifts are not about YOU.
Leadership is not about YOU.
Your purpose is not about YOU.
A life of significance is about SERVING
Those who need your gifts,
Your leadership,
Your purpose.
-Kevin Hall in *Aspire*

"A leader...is like a shepherd.
He stays behind the flock,
Letting the nimble go ahead,
Whereupon the others follow,
Not realizing that all along they are being directed from behind."
-Nelson Mandela

Chapter 9

Building Trust

Stephen Covey is probably best known for his book, "The 7 Habits of Highly Effective People." He wrote another excellent book which states:

> *There is one thing that is common to every individual, relationship, team, family, organization, nation, economy and civilization throughout the world. One thing which, if removed, will destroy the most powerful government, the most successful businesses, the most thriving economy, the most influential leadership, the greatest friendship, the strongest character and the deepest love. On the other hand, if developed and leveraged, that one thing has the potential to create unparalleled success and prosperity in every dimension of life. That one thing is trust.*

Covey's book is entitled, "The Speed of Trust."

Anytime we lower the trust level between us, it begins to negatively impact the opportunity that you and I have to make a difference in the lives of others. If people don't trust the messenger, they're probably not going to adhere to the message. So you and I have to be people of high trust. In 2010, a group did a study of the top characteristics of the most admired leaders.

> ➤ 85 percent said *trustworthy*
> ➤ 70 percent said *visionary*
> ➤ 69 percent said *inspiring* or *motivating*
> ➤ 64 percent said *competent*

Harvard Business Review did an international study and the study showed that the majority of people trust a stranger more than they do their own boss. I struggle with the veracity of that one, but assuming that it's true, it probably explains a lot of the issues that are going on in the marketplace out there.

What God Says about Trust

Read these passages and record for yourself what God says to you about trust.

- *What did Jesus say about trust in Matthew 6:1-8?*
- *Who did He say we should not be like? Why?*
- *What did Jesus say about trusting the spiritual leaders of His day in John 2:23-24?*
- *What did Paul say about the servants of Christ in 1 Corinthians 4:1-2?*
- *What does Proverbs 11:13 say about someone who is trustworthy?*
- *What does Proverbs 12:19 say about truthful lips?*
- *What does Proverbs 14:25 say about a truthful witness?*
- *What does Proverbs 20:6 say about a faithful man?*

- *What advice does Proverbs 20:19 give about gossips?*
- *What does Proverbs 25:14 and 19 say about trusting in a treacherous man?*
- *What advice does Proverbs 25:9-10 give about betraying a confidence?*

My daughter is a civil litigator and is in the courtroom at times. They are trying to verify and determine the credibility of the witness, through what they say, through the events that took place, through their mannerisms, and through corroboration. Ultimately, judgment will be rendered on whether or not they believe this witness. As Christian leaders, we are on the witness stand every day. Everything we say is being inspected and judged. So, it is very important that we are honest, trustworthy, and credible.

Trust may be the most critical thing about any of our relationships and I think it's probably the bedrock of leadership. I would place trust above intelligence, talent, and creativity because if you are not trustworthy, then those things don't matter. You can have all these other things, but if you're not trustworthy they're not going to give themselves to you and allow you to influence them. Trust is really the currency of influence in relationships.

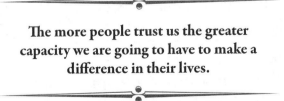

The more people trust us the greater capacity we are going to have to make a difference in their lives.

If we want people to follow or to let us have influence in their lives, they have to trust us. If we want people to trust us, they have to connect with us. If we want people to connect with us, we have to be willing to show them our heart. We have to be willing to be open, transparent, honest, and genuine. We've got to be willing to bleed. We've got to be willing to show vulnerability.

If you've not read Brene Brown's book, "Daring Greatly," you ought to go on YouTube and watch some of her talks on vulnerability. God will use her to get to you about the openness, honesty, vulnerability, transparency, and genuineness of your life. It will be life altering.

Trust Is Built

We want to make a difference. We want to matter. If we're going to make a difference in the lives of folks, it's built on trust. Trust is built and it's earned. It's earned because you've connected with people when you're real. You show them your heart and your life. I wrote down some analogies or word pictures about trust.

Trust is like oil. If you don't have oil in your car engine, everything's going to freeze up and you're not going anywhere. Trust is like that.

Trust is relational money; currency. The more you've got of that, then the more effect that you can have.

Trust is glue. It holds all relationships together.

Everything is built on willingness to trust. Webster's definition of trust says, "Trust is the belief that someone is reliable, good, honest, or effective." Biblically, trust is defined as the willingness to rest your weight on someone.

My guess is all of you trust the chair you're sitting in. Did you pick up the chair, examine the legs, or have a word of prayer before you sat in it? What is interesting is that you probably just basically sat down. You trusted all of your weight to that chair. Even though you may have experienced a chair's collapse in the past, you still generally trust the chair.

I remember years ago, we had an old set of chairs in our dining room and it was a real small area. My seat was up against the pass through wall. I reached back to get something from the pass through and put so much pressure on the chair that it collapsed. Even so, I still sit in chairs and believe they will hold me up. That's trust and that's what we want people to have in each of us. We want them to have the willingness to rest all of their weight on who we are and what we do.

Behaviors that Build Trust

A is able. You build trust when you are competent—you know what to do, how to do it, get it done, and enable others to do the same. People who are able consistently deliver quality results. They're always getting better because they're developing their own skills. They strive to be good at whatever they do. They seek relevant experience. They use their abilities to build others. They never hoard what they have learned.

B is believable. Believable people live and act with integrity of character. You are believable when you listen, when you keep your commitments, when you do what you say you will do when you say you will do it. Believable is when you keep confidences and practice accountability. When you speak the truth, talk straight, and avoid talking behind people's backs, you are believable. When you're sincere, non-judgmental, and show respect for others, you are believable. When you right wrongs, show loyalty, and never take credit for somebody else's work, you are believable.

C is connection or caring. You are truly caring when you listen attentively, praise their efforts, and show genuine interest in them. Be transparent, vulnerable, show empathy, and ask them for input. Never gossip or spread rumors. Do not abuse any authority you might have and never be condescending. People do not care how much you know until they know how much you care.

D   is doing. "Do unto others as you would have them do unto you" (Matthew 7:12; Luke 6:31). Trust is built when you treat others the way that you want to be treated.

E   is extending trust. Showing trust in others helps them to trust you. Being there for people in time of need builds trust. Imagine trust is like a bank account. You've got to keep making deposits if you want the account to grow. When you're able, believable, and connect with people, you make deposits and the account is growing. None of us are perfect and there are going to be times along the way when you don't do what you said you would do or you don't do it when you said you would do it. Even with the purest motives or intents, you sometimes make a withdrawal from that trust account. If you make more withdrawals than deposits, eventually you're bankrupt. You need to continually behave in ways to build that account and then learn how to rebuild trust when it has been lost or damaged.

Behaviors that Rebuild Trust

I recently had lunch with a longtime friend in the church and he said, "Jimmy, I've known you for a long time and I'm going to throw our trust level way up there. Here's what I know from working in the marketplace and dealing with some family issues. At some point, if you don't trust, even in the minimal way, the trust level is going to go down. Though it can be restored to some degree, it's very unlikely that the trust level will ever return to where it originally was. I'm not saying never, because some people have a very unique capacity to do that, but I think those people are rare."

363

It doesn't mean there can't be an element of restoration, but you'll always be a little bit hesitant. You want to, but it's hard to get there. That's why every breach of trust, no matter how small, is significant. You will lose ground that you may never fully recover. That leads me to behaviors that will help rebuild trust.

Admit you messed up. Admit you blew it. Swallow your pride, don't blame someone else, own up, and be responsible. Then look the offended party in the face, and say, "I was wrong and I'm sorry."

Ask for forgiveness. The relationship has been damaged. You need to own up, but to some degree you need to get the onus off of you and onto them. When you ask them to forgive you, you do that. You can't make them forgive you, but it's not your responsibility to do that anyway. Your responsibility is to confess the wrongdoing to God and the person, and then ask them for forgiveness. It's their responsibility whether or not they give it, but if they don't, then they have to deal with the root of bitterness. God will readily forgive, but people sometimes take a little longer.

Act to correct the situation. If there's some kind of needed restitution, do it. This is a very important issue in the restoration of trust. They want to know: How do I know you're not going to do it again? What are you going to do to put in place, to insure with all the fiber of your being that this is not going to happen again?

If these detrimental behaviors are repetitive and to the same person, eventually they get to the point where that person no longer believes you. You've done this a thousand times and you've admitted it, you've asked them to forgive you a thousand times and they have. Here we are at 1,001 and they want to know if you are ever going to stop that behavior. They want to know what action you are going to take to be sure that it's going to be different going forward.

You need to alter whatever the behavior is that continues to disrupt the trust of the relationship and fix it. If that means getting into an accountability group or some other form of help, you need to do whatever it takes to change your behavior and begin to earn back that trust.

In the end, you have to decide who matters the most to you. I don't want to be offensive to anyone, but I want to be least offensive to my wife and kids. One of my definitions of success is I want the people who know me best and love me the most to also respect me the most.

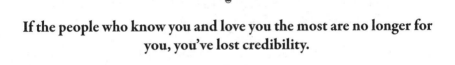

If the people who know you and love you the most are no longer for you, you've lost credibility.

Too many people, including leaders, settle for low trust levels because they don't know how trust is formed. Trust doesn't just happen. It's earned and built through intentional trust building behaviors. Three of the most powerful words anyone can say to you or me in any and all of our relationships are "I trust you." Those are three of the most life altering words not just to hear, but to say.

QUESTIONS FOR SELF REFLECTION
CHAPTER NINE—BUILDING TRUST

1. *In 2010, a group did a study of the top characteristics of the most admired leaders.*

    85 percent said trustworthy

    70 percent said visionary

    69 percent said inspiring or motivating

    64 percent said competent

    Do you agree with this assessment? Why or why not?

2. *From reading the scriptures earlier in the chapter, use a few sentences to summarize what God has said in Scripture about trust.*

    _____

    _____

    _____

3. *We all want to make a difference. We all want to matter. This chapter taught us if we're going to make a difference in the lives of folks, it's built on _____.*

    What do you need to do to build and earn the trust of those who know and love you the most?

    What was your best learning from our study together?

Chapter 10

Helping Others Motivate Themselves

And let us consider how to provoke one another to love and good deeds, not neglecting to meet together, as is the habit of some, but encouraging one another, and all the more as you see the Day approaching.
(Hebrews 10:24-25)

Honestly, we can't motivate anybody to do anything. That's because it is an internal issue. The only person you and I can motivate is the person we see when we look in the mirror. We can motivate ourselves. However, if we understand and know what triggers and motivates us and others, we can create the conditions, the climate, and the environment for them to become more motivated to do the things they ought to do.

A few years ago, I came across a book called, "Get Motivated." I really believe understanding this about yourself is critical in your productivity, enjoyment, and engagement of your own life. Then you can be a motivating factor in the lives of others. The Word of God gives us great insight in this area of motivating ourselves and others. Here are a few to get you started.

Romans 12:11 is one of my favorite verses, "Never flag [lack] in zeal, be aglow with the Spirit, serve the Lord." Stay motivated. Stay on fire. Keep moving. Maintain the fervor.

Hebrews 10:24-25 talks about our responsibility to stir, to stimulate, to motivate one another to do the things that we ought to do.

Then in Acts 2:42, shortly after the church's birth, Luke writes about them being devoted to the apostles' teaching, to fellowship, to the breaking of bread, and to prayer. Devoted is a word we don't use very often, but it means committed and motivated to do the things that God had called them to do.

Motivating Triggers

There are some essential triggers that motivate every one of us. Many of these triggers have to do with competency, being able to get things done, and being able to have freedom and autonomy to decide what to do and how to do it.

Extrinsic Motivation. There are basically two types of triggers that motivate us. One is what I call *extrinsic* which is pressure from the outside. It's not so much the activity that motivates us. It is the possible reward if I do it or the possible punishment if I don't do it. Everything is coming from the outside. It may be I do what I do in order to get the approval of others or I do what I do to avoid the disapproval of my boss. Compensation, financial success, and money for what we do are extrinsic rewards. However, I've learned that when someone is paid fairly for what they do, then money is no longer a motivator for them to do more.

So, the extrinsic things that motivate people to go above and beyond are the approval of others, personal image, job security, an angry boss, and deadlines. In and of themselves, none of these things are bad, but they're only short term in their effect. They can do damage over a period of time, however.

Intrinsic Motivation. What we need to look for is what I call *intrinsic* or more internally motiving triggers. They come more from the inside. Here your behavior is not based on what you'll get if you do it or what you'll get if you don't. You do it for the love of the behavior or the activity. You just love doing it. There are a lot of folks who are making millions of dollars in athletics, but really it isn't a money thing for them. They love the activity. They love the sport. It's the love of engaging in something that you feel like you're good at and you feel makes a difference. Those kind of things really come from the inside.

There are some of us who are self-motivated. Stuff is easier for those who are self-motivated than it is for a lot of other folks. What these people have to watch out for, though, is that sometimes they get whatever it is done, but not for the best of reasons. Sometimes it is to show off, seek the approval of others or to avoid the disapproval of others.

If we're going to motivate ourselves and motivate others, we've got to find something that matters to us and to them. If we can identify those self-interests, then we've got a greater chance of keeping ourselves motivated for the long haul intrinsically and we can motivate others as well.

The Seven Triggers

There are seven triggers that cause us to do what we do and cause us to try to do the best at what we do. These same seven things are what motivates everybody we will talk to the rest of our lives. If we can find out which of these seven most motivate them, and make those things happen at home or at work or in the relationship, then we can do what the writer of Hebrews encouraged us to do. We can stir up one another to love and good deeds.

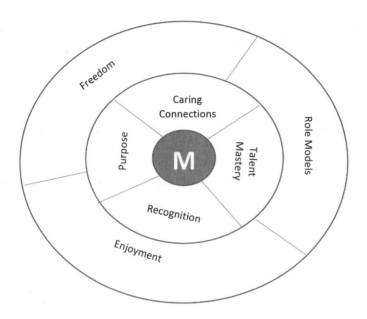

Every one of these is basically an innate, God-given human need. Everybody needs them. Nobody can do without them. When we are without any of these, we get very actively disengaged. We get very demotivated and life, work, and family become drudgery and boredom.

One: Caring Connections. We want to be known, cared for, and know that we matter. We want to know we are more than a number. We want to know that our leader cares about us for who we are and not just for what we can do. We don't want to be a commodity. We want to have meaningful relationships and caring connections. Anonymity demotivates all of us. If we feel like we go to work and no one cares, we get demotivated in a hurry. If our presence doesn't matter, if no one cares if we are there, if we can't add any value by our presence, then we are demotivated.

Two: Talent and Competency. We are motivated when we get to do what we do best and what we enjoy. We are motivated when we are challenged to achieve. We are motivated when we get an opportunity to grow. We're motivated when we get opportunity to develop and add skills and do better at what we're already innately good at.

Those who have the responsibility of supervising and managing must be careful not to beat those we lead up for their non-productivity rather than try to find out how can we better get them motivated and engaged using their God-given talents.

Have you ever asked those you are called to lead what motivates them? It is an essential question. I've done this in sports for years as a coach. I ask them, "How can I best motivate you as a coach?" I know there are only a handful of triggers that can really motivate. The problem is most coaches only have one method; they scream, yell, belittle, and demean. That does work for some kids short term, but that shuts other kids down because of the public embarrassment.

This is a basic question of building meaningful relationships in life. I only asked my wife this question a few years ago and it was part of the reason that I adjusted my at home responsibilities.

My wife said, "You know, Jimmy, just having time with you, not feeling the pressure for it to lead anywhere sexually, just being together. Just sitting in a chair together, sitting at the table together at dinner, talking and not having the television on, doing the dishes together. I treasure those minutes together."

Then after my heart issues, we started having an hour and a half a day walking together. Unbelievable conversation comes out of those times.

Unfortunately, in the work place, they hire you because they think you have a particular talent or skill that can make a contribution at work.

Then they evaluate you on what you're not getting done. If we truly want to lead and motivate others, we need to change this mindset.

Three: Recognition and Affirmation. Being recognized for the contribution you're making at home or at work is a big one for me. I like being appreciated. I like recognition for the contributions and the effort I put forth. Last year 65 percent of the American work force received no praise for what they did. Nobody said, "Thank you." How motivating is that? How difficult is it to say thanks for what you do or we need you? It doesn't take much. If we had more leaders and managers that led this way, we'd have a whole lot more productivity and engagement, longer tenures, and less absenteeism.

Four: Purpose. We want to know how what we do fits into the larger purpose of the organization. That's important to all of us. We want to know what we do really matters. I am particularly adept at this one. I am always reminding them why they're important and why we need them. People want to know that they count.

Five: Freedom. Autonomy, self-determination, the ability to choose to do what they do and how they do it. We'd be a whole lot more productive and better off if we as leaders would say, "Here's what the end goal needs to be. Be sure to talk to me about how you plan to get there, but I'm going to give you a lot of freedom and autonomy to kind of set it out." They get more engaged when they get to determine how to do it than if I just tell them to go robotically and do it my way. People love that sense of self-determination. That doesn't mean there's no accountability, but the more freedom that you give people, the more they earn the freedom because they've done a good job, and the more motivated they are. Autonomy and freedom are critical.

Six: Role Models. They want to see their leaders as people that set the pace and set the example. They are leaders that show up early, stay late, work hard, care, and do what they do best most of the time. I've had two great role models that are motivating to me. I'm challenged by how those guys live and behave. They're not perfect any more than Paul was perfect, but Paul was not ashamed when he said, "Follow me as I follow Christ."

Seven: When work is fun. I've got the greatest job in the whole world. I've never looked elsewhere. I've been here for many years. I love what I do. I love the people I get to work with. We laugh together, we joke together, we cry together and when heartache takes place, it's like a family. We enjoy working and being together.

Don't Assume People Know What Motivates You

Research at Duke University and George Mason University reveals that although you might think you know what motivates your people, you probably don't. At regular intervals over a forty year period, executives, bosses, managers, and leaders were asked to rank what they thought motivated their employees. They consistently got it wrong.

Executives erroneously believed that external factors and incentives such as compensation, bonuses, job security, and promotion are what most motivated their employees. However, employees reported that internal factors such as interesting work, being appreciated, making meaningful contributions, a feeling of being involved in the decision, and being part of something bigger are what motivated them the most.

However, employees were no better predicting what motivated their bosses and peers. They got it wrong, too. They believed it was external factors that motivated their superiors. The fact is executives reported being motivated mostly by autonomy, their inherent interest in their work, how they handle challenges, and a sense of relatedness with their colleagues.

This research shows we don't know what our bosses want. We don't know what our peers want and they don't know what we want. We all tend to think it's just simply more money and more rewards, but it really isn't. The same is true with our spouses and our friends. Unless we share with each other what motivates us and ask what motivates them, we will probably never figure it out.

We assume people know what motivates us, but odds are we're wrong in both directions most of the time. You have to tell them. Discover what motivates the people you love, know, and work with. You will be very glad you did.

Here are seven questions we ought to ask ourselves at least once a week concerning the people that we're spending most of our time with. These are critical, important questions.

1. *Who will I really care about this week? Get intentional. If you work in an office with eight or nine people, pick one out a week and try to build a relationship.*
2. *Who will I challenge to grow and achieve this week?*
3. *Who will I recognize and affirm this week?*
4. *How will I connect with someone and explain the larger purpose of what they do in our organization or family?*
5. *Who will I help to have more freedom to do what they do well this week?*
6. *What do I need to do to model for others?*

7. What can I do to inject some fun and enjoyment this week at home or in the office?

Practical Steps You Can Take

Intentionally position yourself to experience your prime intrinsic motivations. If you know what they are, you are foolish not to do everything that's in your power and control to make all of those you interact with in life know these things about you. You are wrong to assume they know.

Know who, what, when, and where best energizes and drains you. There are certain people who motivate and energize me when I'm around them. There are also certain people that suck the life out of me when I'm around them. There are certain things that I do that energize and motivate me, but there are certain things that drain the life out of me. I know the environment, the culture, and the conditions when I am most energized, drained, and productive.

Hire people who do their job, keep them motivated to do their job, and get out of the way and let them do their job. If they're not doing the job, tell them why and try to help them fix it. If they don't get it fixed, fire them.

Protect your personal margin. Rest, exercise, and eat well. When you're tired and worn out, you're going to be lethargic and unmotivated. You will not be able to help motivate others when you are not running on full power.

Stay connected with God. It's one of the most important discoveries about your journey you will ever make. You need to know how you best connect with God.[1] Associate with motivated people. They are contagious.

---

[1] If you go to www.firstorlando.com/about/membership, there's a spiritual pathways assessment available that will really peg how you best connect with God.

Resources

Over the years, I have found three great resources you can go to on motivation. They have proven to be very valuable to me as I have tried to gain a better understanding on this important subject of motivation.

1. **Daniel Pink's** *New York Times* bestseller, "Drive: The Surprising Truth About What Motivates Us." If you don't want to read the book, just go to YouTube and type in Daniel Pink and there are hundreds of videos by Daniel talking about what motivates us as human beings. He's not a believer, but this is a really good book.

2. **Pat Lencioni**, is another one you can access on YouTube. One of his best books is a parable about an office situation and the title of the book is, "The Three Signs of a Miserable Job." He's hilarious and entertaining.

3. **James Robbins**, a business consultant, has a book entitled, "Nine Minutes on Monday." An excellent work for helping motivate others.

When it's all over with and you retire, you resign, or you go to another job, you'll have a legacy and it won't have anything to do with your work. They'll remember less about how great a worker you were and remember more about the great person you were.

QUESTIONS FOR SELF REFLECTION
CHAPTER TEN—HELPING OTHERS MOTIVATE
THEMSELVES

1. *There are some essential triggers that motivate every one of us. Many of these triggers have to do with competency, being able to get things done, and being able to have freedom and autonomy to decide what to do and how to do it. There are basically two types of triggers that motivate us. What are your specific Extrinsic Motivators? What are your specific Intrinsic Motivators?*

2. *Do you know who, what, when, and where best energizes and drains you? List each one here.*

3. *Do you protect your personal margin? Do you rest, exercise, and eat well? Do you stay connected with God? Do you associate with motivated people?*

4. *If you answered no to any of these questions, what are you going to do to change that so you can help motivate others?*

5. *Following are seven questions we addressed that you ought to ask ourselves at least once a week concerning the people we are spending most of our time with. Use this as your own personal check list.*

   ❑ *Who will I really care about this week?*

   ❑ *Who will I challenge to grow and achieve this week?*

   ❑ *Who will I recognize and affirm this week?*

   ❑ *How will I connect with someone and explain the larger purpose of what they do in our organization or family?*

   ❑ *Who will I help to have more freedom to do what they do well this week?*

   ❑ *What do I need to do to model for others?*

   ❑ *What can I do to inject some fun and enjoyment this week at home or in the office?*

6. *What was your best learning from this chapter?*

Chapter 11

Living and Leading with Greater Wisdom

If any of you lacks wisdom, let him ask God, who gives to all men generously
and without reproaching, and it will be given him. But let him ask in faith,
with no doubting, for he who doubts is like a wave of the sea that is driven and
tossed by the wind. For that person must not suppose that a double-minded
man, unstable in all his ways, will receive anything from the Lord.
(James 1:5-8 RSV)

Regretful, ashamed, stupid, grieved, and broken are feelings we all have had, but I don't think anyone plans to mess up his or her life. None of us get up one day and plan to make an ignorant, life-changing decision. So how do we avoid making unwise decisions and begin to live and lead with greater wisdom?

One of the most important questions we should ask before making any potential life-changing decision is, "What is the wise thing to do?" I think many of my bad decisions would have been aborted if I'd asked that question. I encourage you to incorporate it into your life, into your thinking, and into your experiences.

Much of what we do is stepping into the unknown. One of the things I have found myself doing more in the last five to ten years is really asking the Lord for wisdom. I don't need to try to impress anybody with intellect, academics, knowledge or anything else. What I really need is God's wisdom. When I don't know what I'm walking into, I know that God does so I ask Him to speak to my heart and mind and to bring out whatever is necessary in terms of wisdom to make the right decision in what I do and say.

Ephesians 5:1-3 says, "Therefore be imitators of God, as beloved children. And walk in love, as Christ loved us and gave himself up for us, a fragrant offering and sacrifice to God. But immorality and impurity or covetousness must not even be named among you, as not fitting among the saints." Paul then gives us a list of things not to do in life. In verses 15-17 he says, "Look carefully then how you walk, not as unwise men but as wise, making the most of the time, because the days are evil. Therefore do not be foolish, but understand what the will of the Lord is." That is a profound statement because it means we do ultimately have a choice. We need to learn from our experiences, from life, from the Scriptures, and from others in our decision-making process.

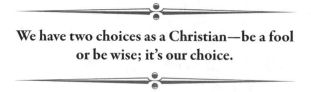

We have two choices as a Christian—be a fool or be wise; it's our choice.

Seeking to understand the will of the Lord could be equated with seeking wisdom. That word *understand* is an interesting word. I think what Paul is saying here is don't be a fool, but understand where true wisdom lies. James 3:13-16 draws a comparison between godly wisdom and ungodly wisdom or the world's wisdom. There is a huge contrast between the two types of wisdom.

Who is wise and understanding among you? By his good life let him show his works in meekness of wisdom. But if you have bitter jealousy and selfish ambition in your hearts, do not boast and be false to the truth. This is not the wisdom that comes down from above, but is earthly, unspiritual, and demonic. For where jealousy and selfish ambition exist, there will be disorder, chaos, confusion, and every vile and evil practice. The wisdom from above is first pure, then peaceable, gentle, open to reason, full of mercy and good fruits, without uncertainty or insincerity and a harvest of righteousness is sown in peace by those who make peace.

We're constantly making decisions about which way we'll go. Even if we think we are not making a conscious decision, we are choosing. If we unpack these verses, James contrasts the origin of wisdom saying it is either from below or from above. The qualities that define wisdom from above will lead us in the right direction; wisdom from below always leads us in the wrong way. The results achieved are in stark contrast to each other. The thing we need to realize is we get to choose. No one makes the choice for us.

Wisdom is the application of knowledge combined with discernment, understanding, obedience, insight, experience, talent, and education. They all work together to help us make wise decisions. It's the ability to practically apply what we have learned so that we can live the kind of life that's pleasing to God. Ultimately, we can't separate godly wisdom and godly character. Godly character shaped by the fruit of the Spirit is what produces wisdom in our lives and what leads us to please God. Where do we find godly wisdom?

Biblical Facts about Wisdom

Wisdom is available. Wisdom is personified in Proverbs 1:20-21, "Wisdom cries out in the street, in the market places she raises her voice; on the top of the walls she cries out; at the entrance of the city gates she speaks." In other words, wisdom is screaming, "I'm here, I'm available."

Wisdom can be rejected. "How long, O simple ones, will you love being simple?" The idea of simple is they don't know what they need. "How long will scoffers delight in their scoffing?" Scoffers think they know all the answers and don't need anybody's help. "Fools hate knowledge." They don't just misuse it, but neither do they seek it. "Give heed to my reproof, behold, I will pour out my thoughts to you and I will make my words known to you. Because I have called to you and you have refused to listen, have stretched out my hand and no one has heeded, you have ignored all my counsel and would have none of my reproof" (Proverbs 1:22-25).

Rejecting wisdom has consequences. Notice the results we get if we reject wisdom. "I will laugh at your calamity; I will mock when panic strikes you. When panic strikes you like a storm and your calamity comes like a whirlwind, when distress and anguish come upon you. Then they will call upon me, but I will not answer; they will seek me diligently but will not find me. Because they hated knowledge and did not choose the fear of the Lord, would have none of my counsel and despised all my reproof" (Proverbs 1:26-28). Reject wisdom and there are consequences that can sometimes be life altering.

"The fear of the Lord is the beginning of wisdom" (Proverbs 1:29-33). The fear of the Lord is recognizing who God is and it's also recognizing who we aren't. It's revering and submitting to who God is.

Why Don't We Get It?

Wisdom is available. God wants us to have it. So, why do we miss it and go on to make bad or unwise decisions?

Number One: We tend to be emotional people. Many of our regretful stories and the decisions we have made were in the context of relationships, a time of crisis, and when we were emotionally charged. One of the reasons we miss the wisdom that's available is because we let our emotions take over and rule our minds. We said or did something in the emotion of the moment that we now regret.

Number Two: We lack knowledge or expertise, but we didn't know it. It's like the fool who doesn't know what he doesn't know. We don't think we need anybody's help. I'm not a financial expert. What I should have done instead of trying to make a financial decision on my own was make a few phone calls and get the help and advice I needed to make a wise decision. Health-wise I also ignored heart issues for ten days thinking I knew what was going on and it almost killed me. Wise leaders must be willing to humble themselves and to be teachable. Wisdom is researching and networking to locate those who can provide expert input so wise decisions can be made.

Number Three: We choose not to heed the Spirit of God. We know it's the Spirit of God or the wise thing to do, but we just choose not to do it.

Leading a Life with Greater Wisdom

Now, I don't think there's any magic formula for living and leading with greater wisdom, but I do think there are some key elements that need to be there if you and I are going to live and lead more wisely.

Pursue godly wisdom. Proverbs 2:4 says, "If you seek it like silver and search for it as hidden treasures." I think what the writer of Proverbs is trying to help us to see is that wisdom is not fast food. If we want to be a person of wisdom, we have to search for it intently and deliberately seek it as we would a valuable treasure. Real godly wisdom is not accidently found. It's something we go after. It's something we pursue over power, position or financial security.

Pray for it. James 1:5 says, "If anyone lacks wisdom, let him ask God." We need to backtrack and read this in the context of verses 2-4. "Count it all joy, my brothers, when you meet various trials.

For you know the testing, the trials of your faith produces steadfastness...that you may become mature, perfect, lacking in nothing. If anyone lacks wisdom..." What James is saying is if anybody lacks wisdom in time of pain, difficulty, and trial, ask for it. When we ask for it then God provides it for us. Solomon asked God for wisdom and God gave it to him and commended him for asking for it. Wisdom would be a good thing to pray for, especially in times of difficulty. In fact when we come to God and ask for wisdom, especially in times of difficulty and pain or heartache, God doesn't give it begrudgingly or sparingly. God graciously and generously gives wisdom, not judging us because He is pleased we know we need it. God knows we don't have the wisdom that we need, but all too often we choose to rely on our own human wisdom and our own intellect instead of admitting we need His help.

Study and obey the Scriptures. Psalm 119:98-100 talks about the Scriptures being a source of wisdom. When we're reading Scripture, we should be looking for the principles that are applicable to our life situation. There are an enormous amount of the issues and experiences of life that are not specifically addressed in Scripture, but principles are laid there to guide us in the right direction. If we heed the wisdom of God as we know it, then we will know the wisdom of God when we need it. If we're living, doing, and fleshing out the wisdom and the will of God as we clearly know it in our lives on a regular basis, then when the unexpected comes up and the need for wisdom arises, God is more likely to supply just what we need right when we need it.

Practice rigorous, self-evaluation. We are masters at the art of self-deception and denial. We don't know what we don't know and a lot of what we do know is wrong. I'm huge on self-awareness and seeking to know how God has put each of us together. How God has put us together identifies both strengths and weaknesses, as well as blind spots and temptation areas in our lives so we can use them to our advantage. If we know those things about ourselves, then they can become wisdom producers in our lives. If we don't know where we are strong, talented, capable, as well as where we are incompetent and where our blind spots are, we will be susceptible to temptation and are basically going in blind. If we aren't aware of what's working and what's not working in our lives then we don't know what we need to walk away from and what we need to walk toward, so we will wander around aimlessly. We will probably make unwise decisions since we really have no clear direction.

We all have areas in our lives where we need wisdom. Those areas need to be identified so we can get the help we need whether it is financial, medical, life or relational.

We are professional self-deceivers, and we don't like it when somebody speaks truth about us that we don't agree with. We need to be able to look in the mirror and tell ourselves the truth. Only then can we become wisdom producers.

Heed feedback and counsel. Proverbs 1:5, 11:14, 12:15, 15:22, and 19:20 are all about feedback and counsel. When we get feedback from somebody else, it's always addressing the past. Counsel or advice is always addressing the future. We need both. We need the rearview mirror and we need the windshield in order to move forward safely and productively. We're not good at giving ourselves feedback because of self-deception. All of us need reliable advisors who resemble a personal board of directors and will speak the truth in love to us, and not only what we want to hear.

Proverbs gives us the contrast between a person of wisdom and a fool. There is one common glaring difference between a person who is wise and a person who is a fool. The wise person listens to feedback and counsel. Wise leaders also heed the feedback and counsel they receive. They don't shift the blame and responsibility to anybody else. They embrace the feedback and counsel and make the necessary changes to get it right. The fool doesn't. A fool rationalizes and does not change what needs to be changed.

I think one of the greatest things that I've read in years is Chapter 7 of Henry Cloud's book, "Necessary Endings." Chapter 7 is entitled, "The Wise, the Foolish, and the Evil." If we want to affect change, we have to deal with all three. However, we cannot treat a fool the same way we treat a wise person or an evil person.

Associate with wise people. Proverbs 13:20 says, "He who walks with wise men becomes wise, but the companion of fools will suffer harm." Draw from their experience. If we work in a difficult office where there is constant profanity, foolishness, and evil that pounds us eight hours a day, five days a week, it's hard to dismiss that influence. It gets in our heart and minds even though we don't want it to, so we have to counter balance it with what happens at home, at church, in our Bible reading, and our prayer life. If we don't counter it, it will drain and suck the life out of us.

Develop a habit of asking one of life's greatest questions. What is the wise thing to do? **Wisdom takes time.** It's a process. It's not fast food.

Rewards of Seeking Wisdom

- Proverbs 1:33 says, "But he who listens to Me will dwell secure and will be at ease without dread or evil."
- Proverbs 3:21 says, "My son, keep sound wisdom and discretion, let them not escape from your sight for they will be life for your soul and adornment for your neck. Then you will walk on your way securely, and your foot will not stumble. If you sit down you will not be afraid; if you lie down your sleep will be sweet. Do not be afraid of sudden panic or the ruin of the wicked when it comes for the Lord will be your confidence and will keep your foot from being caught."
- James 3:13 says, "Who is wise and understanding among you? By his good life..."
- James 3:18 says, "And a harvest of righteousness is sown in peace by those who make peace."
- Proverbs 28:26 says, "He who trusts in his own mind is a fool, but he who walks in wisdom will be delivered."

Seeking Wisdom Brings...

- **a good life.** Who doesn't want a good life that is full, enjoyable, beautiful, attractive, and winsome? I think most folks want that, but it has to be pursued. God will not just drop it in your lap.

- **internal peace.** When you and I walk in wisdom with God, there is a quiet, inner peace and confidence that we will have what we need when we need it.

- **external fruit.** James 3:18 talks about a fruit of righteousness. In other words, wisdom, character, and integrity are inseparable. We live a life that's like Christ in attitudes, beliefs, and behaviors. These are products of wisdom and help produce more of the same in our lives.

- **security and comfort.** Wisdom instills security and comfort as a way of life whether it is sunny or stormy.

- **deliverance.** It brings deliverance from having regrets, heartaches, and unnecessary pain because of unwise decisions.

Wisdom is available.
We have to search for it, diligently seek it, and
go after it like we would a buried treasure;
but there are rich rewards when it is found and applied.

One of the things that has dramatically improved in my life is the willingness to know what I don't know, go to people that I think do know, and ask for help in the areas where I want to know. It's not just finding wisdom, it's having the fortitude and the courage to act on it and that's not easy. Growing in wisdom is a lifelong pursuit. It's always pursuing and never arriving, so be a wisdom seeker. Decide today to walk and grow toward wisdom.

I pray Ephesians 1:17 over you: "May the God of our Lord Jesus Christ, the Father of glory, give you a spirit of wisdom and of revelation in the knowledge of Him." I don't know that I could pray anything more needful or effective over your life.

QUESTIONS FOR SELF REFLECTION
CHAPTER ELEVEN—LIVING AND LEADING WITH
GREATER WISDOM

1. *How do you avoid making unwise decisions and begin to live and lead with greater wisdom?*

2. *James 3:13-16 draws a comparison between godly wisdom and ungodly wisdom or the world's wisdom. What did you learn from this comparison?*

3. *Wisdom is the application of knowledge combined with _____, _____, _____, _____, _____, _____, and _____. Do you use them all to help you make wise decisions? Do you practically apply what you have learned so that you can live the kind of life that's pleasing to God?*

4. *Ultimately, we can't separate godly wisdom and godly character. Godly character shaped by the fruit of the Spirit is what produces wisdom in our lives and what leads us to please God. Where do you find this godly wisdom?*

5. *Wisdom is available. God wants us to have it. What did you discover that causes you to miss it and make bad or unwise decisions?*

6. *Develop a habit of asking one of life's greatest questions. What is that question?*

7. *Jimmy said: "It's not just finding wisdom; it's also having _____."*

8. *What was your best learning from this chapter?*

Chapter 12

Building Healthy Teams

After WWII, a general and a young lieutenant boarded a train in London at the train station. They were running late and by the time they boarded the train there were only two seats left on the train. So they took those two seats. Those two seats were directly across from a grandmother and her beautiful granddaughter. Not too long after the train left the station, it went through a tunnel and was in total darkness for about ten to fifteen seconds. As the train was making its way through the tunnel, there were two sounds that were heard—a kiss and a slap. When they exited the tunnel, everybody had their perspective of what maybe happened. The beautiful granddaughter thought to herself, *I'm really kind of flattered that young lieutenant kissed me, but I'm a little bit embarrassed that my grandmother slapped him.*

The grandmother's perspective was, *I can't believe that young lieutenant kissed my granddaughter, but I am so proud of her for retaliating and slapping him.*

Then there was the general who thought to himself, *My young lieutenant showed a lot of courage. I'm really proud of him, but I don't understand why she slapped me.*

There was only one person on that train that knew exactly what had happened in those few seconds. That young lieutenant seized the moment and seized the opportunity to do two things. Kiss the pretty girl and slap his general.

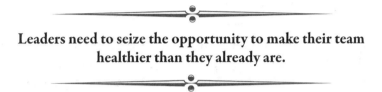

Leaders need to seize the opportunity to make their team healthier than they already are.

There's no way we can have any discussion on leadership without understanding we must build healthy leaders, managers, and other key players on our teams.

When I look back on my life, I see that it is simply scattered and spattered with one team after another. Whether it was with sports teams, small group teams in school, clubs that I was part of, a foursome that I played with every Wednesday, Saturday or Sunday, or the small task force I was part of at DuPont, I was never doing it alone. There's always been a team.

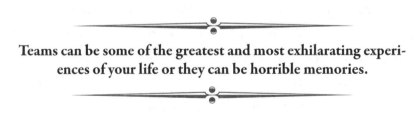

Teams can be some of the greatest and most exhilarating experiences of your life or they can be horrible memories.

A team leader can make or break their team. The first thing we need to be aware of is there is always room for growth and greater health. There is never a sense that we need to feel we have arrived. What I have found most interesting though is the difference in the perspectives between the managers and the team members. Managers and leaders tend to look at things through rose colored glasses. They always hope it's better than it actually is. Reality is what the folks on the line are saying. There tends to be a huge gap in terms of where the leader thinks they are and where they really want to be as a team.

No matter how smart, how competent, how capable, how talented, how intelligent, how trained, how experienced each person on the team is individually, you are better in all of those ways as a team.

Healthy vs. Unhealthy Teams

The concept that we are better as a team is a hard one to develop in the culture in which we live today. Never has our society and culture more encouraged me-ism, being an island, and being a loner than it does now. However, we can never be our best self by ourselves. Whether our team is family or friends or co-workers, we need people that can speak into our lives to make us better individuals. To begin this discovery process, let's look at the attitudes and actions that make teams low performing, failing teams, and then find some common threads that make a team exceptional and high performance.

What makes a team unhealthy? Of course, me-ism is at the top of the list. This mindset causes selfishness and a *me first* versus *we first* attitude. Since it is ego-driven, it causes withholding information from the team because they know knowledge is power rather than sharing it and empowering others. Then there is the pessimist who is always complaining and brings negativity and a critical spirit into the team dynamics. That doesn't mean that you can't have a justifiable criticism, but there's a time and a place and a way to do it that's appropriate and is constructive not destructive to the team. Stubbornness is the fruit of both of these symptoms of an unhealthy team. They feel it is my way or the highway and are hard headed with a fixed mindset that refuses to even consider any other way of doing things.

One of the most dangerous is what I call defensiveness. It is self-protection and shows up in shifting the blame. It is never "my" fault; always somebody else's fault. It can manifest as anger, volatility, and lashing out when they don't get their way.

Be a Healthy Team Leader

What makes a team healthy? **Clarity is a big factor.** When everybody knows what they're supposed to do, knows how to do it, and then performs their job, then there is success for the whole team. There needs to be clarity in the area of vision and standards as well. When you've got five visions and everybody's got a different agenda and a different end in mind, the team will be ineffective. The whole team needs to be committed to the common vision, standards and values.

This leads into the next characteristic of a healthy team and that is **selflessness**. There needs to be a genuine interest in developing each other's strengths and growing each other. This develops from a mutual respect and trust of one another.

However, the most important requirement for a healthy team is a **healthy team leader**. If the person that is leading others and managing the team is not mentally, emotionally, psychologically mature and healthy, they will have trouble creating a healthy team and leading others effectively. We can't lead others where we have not been and where we are not going.

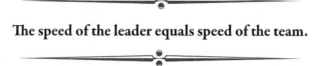

The speed of the leader equals speed of the team.

Our role as a leader is to add value to the lives of our team members. If we cannot say *follow me* to our team and mean it, then we've got a big problem.

As team leaders, we each need to ask ourselves if we can honestly say:

- *Follow my values.*
- *Follow my integrity.*
- *Follow my work ethics.*
- *Follow my commitment.*
- *Follow my communication patterns.*
- *Fight as I fight.*
- *Focus as I focus.*
- *Sacrifice as I sacrifice.*
- *Love as I love.*
- *Admit when you are wrong as I admit when I am wrong.*
- *Endure hardship as I endure hardship.*

When requisite actions back them up, these are the words that set followers' hearts toward you. You've got to set the pace. You need to know your stuff. You need to be knowledgeable and competent. You don't necessarily have to be an expert, but you need to be moving in that direction. Are you more competent and knowledgeable today about what you do than you were a year ago? If not, you're stagnant. The danger for high competency people is that they get to a plateau and they stay there. You've got to keep moving forward and be teachable. Nobody can push you more than you need to be pushing yourself. It's not often talked about in our world today, but we also need to be vulnerable, transparent, and open.

As a leader, I am always asking myself two questions. *Would these men and women willingly follow me if I did not have the power to reward or discipline them?* There's a significant difference in having a following and being worth following. You want to be the second one. You don't want people to do what you tell them because of where they sit on the organizational chart. You want them to follow you because they respect and trust your knowledge and your work ethics.

Then a second question that needs to be asked is, *Am I in it for them or for myself?* Is this all about me? If it's the latter, they will know you're using them and they'll do their job, but they'll never do it with the excellence and attitude they could if they knew you were for the betterment of the team. **Select healthy teammates.** You get the right leadership that's healthy and you bring on the team folks that are healthy, it's going to be a winning, productive, high performance, exceptional team. Teammate selection is probably 60-80 percent of an organization's success. People decisions are your most important decisions. My suggestion about teammates is hire around your limitations and weaknesses. We all have deficiencies. If you're a smart leader, you'll hire for your deficiencies. If you're smart, you hire people who are smarter, more productive, and more talented than you are. Most people don't do that because they're insecure.

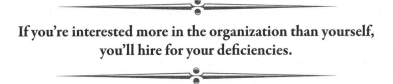

If you're interested more in the organization than yourself, you'll hire for your deficiencies.

Next, hire people who bring character, competency, and chemistry to your team. Character is the most important thing about who we are. It determines what we do in our attitude and it's something that most of us rarely ever examine. We talk about our IQ and our EQ, but what about our CQ, our character quotient? A lot of times, those character gaps or holes are what I call blind spots. You know what a blind spot is in your automobile when you look in the side mirror. We all have those in our lives and need to become aware of them.

Don't treat all teammates the same because they aren't. Some are more productive, some are smarter, some are more effective, and some are more efficient so treat them that way. They deserve it.

If you want to win, pick winners. Hire thoroughbreds, not jackasses because there's a significant difference between the two. Hire attitude, heart, and character above talent. Never hire anyone you would avoid on your day off.

Everyone on the team has got to embrace what I call a **common and shared vision and values**. Vision is where the team is going. Values are how the team plans to act while they go there. If there's a lack of vision and value, the team is missing direction, purpose, and commitment. When people have a common and shared vision and values, they link their arms together and they move forward. However, when everybody has their own personal agenda, their own personal vision, and their own set of personal values, they're always working against one another.

Keep each team member **motivated**. Don't assume what motivates the team members is a pay check. What really counts over the long haul is intrinsic, it comes from the inside of us. We have addressed the seven things that motivate people to come back every day.

Do the people that I work for and work with care about me first and foremost as a person?

Do I have clarity about what my role and responsibilities are and where they fit into the bigger picture of what we're trying to do?

Am I getting better at what I'm doing? Am I mastering my craft and my skill?

Am I having fun with the people that I work with and who I work for?

Am I fairly financially compensated?

Do I have a high degree of freedom to learn, to grow, to fail, and to give my best?

Am I micro managed or do I have autonomy?

Healthy teams foster **genuine care for one another** as team members. Genuine care starts with the leader because as goes the leader, so goes the rest of the team as well. Leaders who focus on relationships build trust. If you want people to follow you, they have to trust you. If you want people to trust you, they have to connect with you. If you want people to connect with you, you have to be willing to show them your heart. If you show people your heart, you will connect with them at the most important level and trust goes off the chart. Then they're willing to follow you wherever you want to go.

Here are some short powerful statements that should be coming out of your mouth on a regular basis:

"Thank you."

"My fault."

"I'm sorry."

"Great job."

"I trust you."

These statements really build relationships so use them often.

A **genuine sense of community** separates good teams from great teams. Everybody's dealing with something. We've all got baggage and we need to treat each other as if we know that.

Create a safe place for conflict and failure. Conflict and failure sharpen every member of the team. When there is a fear of conflict and you're afraid to confront, it is an evidence of an absence of trust.

Encourage risk taking. Team unity is not the absence of conflict; it's the presence of a forgiving spirit. You'll never take a risk to avoid failure which means you'll never get better if it is lacking. Welcome opinions and welcome diversity. You're going to have conflict so always attack the problem and not the people. Don't make it personal or you'll damage the relationship.

Maintain a sustainable pace. A leader needs to know the capacity of everybody on their team. They don't all have the same capacity.

Avoid burnout. Don't overload yourself or others for too long or it will catch up with you. Create margins and flexible schedules. Help the people on the team to find their rhythm.

Provide evaluation and accountability. Accountability and evaluation should be about improvement, growth, and development. It's about getting better. I'm amazed at how we hire people for what they can do and then end up evaluating them in performance reviews for what they didn't do. Did they do well what you hired them to do? If they didn't, that's a whole different thing. Focus on the individual's strengths over their weaknesses. Help develop their strengths. If somebody is in peril of being disciplined or losing their job, it should not be a surprise. Have evaluations and regular conversations along the way.

Work hard to measure outcome and results over processes.

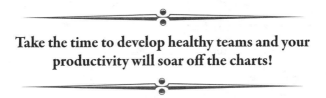

Rejoice in their successes and encourage them in their struggles. Share credit for wins and take blame for losses. That's what leaders do. Don't pass the buck.

Great teams enjoy life together outside the work place. **Have fun together away from work.**

Take the time to develop healthy teams and your productivity will soar off the charts!

QUESTIONS FOR SELF REFLECTION
CHAPTER TWELVE—BUILDING HEALTHY TEAMS

1. *Teams can be some of the greatest and most exhilarating experiences of your life or they can be horrible memories. Which was it for you?*

2. *No matter how smart, how competent, how capable, how talented, how intelligent, how trained, how experienced each person on the team is individually, you are better in all of those ways as a team. Do you agree or disagree? Explain your answer.*

3. *What makes a team unhealthy? Are you doing or allowing any of these things within your team?*

4. *What makes a team healthy? Which ones do you need to start doing for your team?*

5. *As a team leader, ask yourself if you can honestly say:*

- *Follow my values.*
- *Follow my integrity.*
- *Follow my work ethics.*
- *Follow my commitment.*
- *Follow my communication patterns.*
- *Fight as I fight.*
- *Focus as I focus.*
- *Sacrifice as I sacrifice.*
- *Love as I love.*
- *Admit when you are wrong as I admit when I am wrong.*
- *Endure hardship as I endure hardship.*

Which ones do you need to work on?

6. *Ask yourself:*

   Would the men and women on my team willingly follow me if I did not have the power to reward or discipline them?

   Do I truly rejoice in their successes and encourage them in their struggles?

   Do I share credit for wins and take blame for losses?

   Am I doing my best to develop a healthy team?

7. *What was your best learning from this chapter?*

Chapter 13

Success God's Way

Then Moses summoned Joshua, and said to him in the sight of all Israel, "Be strong and of good courage; for you shall go with this people into the land which the LORD has sworn to their fathers to give them; and you shall put them in possession of it. It is the LORD who goes before you; he will be with you, he will not fail you or forsake you; do not fear or be dismayed." And the LORD commissioned Joshua the son of Nun and said, "Be strong and of good courage; for you shall bring the children of Israel into the land which I swore to give them: I will be with you."
(Deuteronomy 31:7-8, 23)

God had raised up Moses to lead the Hebrew nation and as they came close to entering the Promised Land, a sin that had haunted Moses all of his journey, the sin of uncontrollable anger manifested. He lashed out in anger yet another time, but this time at God. He struck a rock. God forgave him, but the consequence of that was God said, "You're not going to lead My people into the Promised Land." God chose Joshua to be Moses' successor and to lead the people into the Promised Land.

After the death of Moses the servant of the Lord, the Lord said to Joshua the son of Nun, Moses' assistant, "Moses my servant is dead. Now therefore arise, go over this Jordan, you and all this people, into the land that I am giving to them, to the people of Israel. Every place that the sole of your foot will tread upon I have given to you, just as I promised to Moses. From the wilderness and this Lebanon as far as the great river, the river Euphrates, all the land of the Hittites to the Great Sea toward the going down of the sun shall be your territory. No man shall be able to stand before you all the days of your life. Just as I was with Moses, so I will be with you. I will not leave you or forsake you. Be strong and courageous, for you shall cause this people to inherit the land that I swore to their fathers to give them. Only be strong and very courageous, being careful to do according to all the law that Moses my servant commanded you. Do not turn from it to the right hand or to the left, that you may have good success wherever you go. This Book of the Law shall not depart from your mouth, but you shall meditate on it day and night, so that you may be careful to do according to all that is written in it. For then you will make your way prosperous, and then you will have good success. Have I not commanded you? Be strong and courageous. Do not be frightened, and do not be dismayed, for the Lord your God is with you wherever you go."
(Joshua 1:1-9)

I received a book written by Michael Kendrick entitled "God's Blueprint for Life. Discovering the Reason that You Were Born." The opening paragraph of the third chapter of the book is: "God's Blueprint for Success."

We live in a world that tells us constantly what's important and what we ought to be striving for. It promises that we can have a fulfilling

*life if we hang out with the right people, if we drive the right car, if we
wear the right clothes, if we drink the right beer, if we find security in
the right insurance, if we exude the right scent and on and on and on.
But what if we strive after this kind of life and find out later that we
were really being measured by other criteria? What if we're competing
with one set of standards in mind while another set of standards was
more important? What if we're pursuing the wrong things?*

A number of years ago, I met a man who was in the interviewing process to become the new senior pastor of our church. I was very uncomfortable in my spirit about this man becoming the new leader of the church, but it was not a decision for me to make. I was simply to pray for those that were making it. Easter was his first Sunday there, and I was to meet him up in the office concourse where our offices were and then we were going to walk down the concourse together and down the back stairwell and make our way to the worship center before Easter services. We met, made our way down the stairwell, got down to just above the first floor, and then he stopped.

He turned around to face me and said, "Jimmy, if you will stay with me, I promise you I will take you to the top."

Back then I was much younger, brasher, and not so smart at times.

I looked at him and said, "I'm afraid your ladder is leaning against the wrong wall."

He was climbing a ladder called success which is a ladder many chase every day. However, many will sacrifice just about anything and everything, even things of great value, in order to achieve it. It's something that we don't consciously think about pursuing and achieving, but it is one of the motivating factors for why we get up every day. We are striving to succeed in some area of our life. It is a critically important subject because it impacts everything about us.

Even though Scripture doesn't use the word success too frequently, it uses the word *prosper* or *prosperous* a number of times. The concept of success is replete in the Bible. How you and I view success, how we define it, and how we think it ought to be measured influences who we are, what we do, why we do what we do, and what we become. Every facet of our lives is impacted by how we view success, yet it's something we rarely talk about.

If you watch Christian television, you might hear the terms prosperity, health, and wealth, but from a biblical perspective, teaching on success as God measures and defines it is rare.

We are climbing the ladder of success, so we must be sure it's leaning against the correct wall.

That wall is God's view and definition of success and how He measures it. That's the only way to find personal fulfillment in our own life and be a blessing to others around us.

How we personally define and measure success determines how we answer these three questions.

Is it permissible for a Christian to pursue success?
Can a Christian live a godly life and pursue success simultaneously: Are they compatible concepts or are they contradictory?
Is God interested in our success?

God's Definition of Success

Not only is our God interested in our success, He's fully committed to the success of His people. If you read about the lives of Joseph, Daniel, David, Moses, Nehemiah, and Joshua there is no doubt that God was committed to their being successful His way. God is just as committed to you and me being successful as long as it's His way and according to His definition. There are at least three evidences that God is really committed to you and me being successful.

First, He gives us principles to guide us. There are hundreds of thousands of books available on how to be a success. Even though each author puts their own spin on success, the same basic fundamental principles always rise to the top defining what a person must be and do in order to be successful. Behind every one of those principles is a biblical principle. The author may be secular and disinterested in the things of God, but the principles are there in His Word so that we can experience success His way.

The second evidence is He creates within each of us a passion to pursue success. It's innate. We're born that way. Watch children and you will see that if they can't get something done or they feel they are failing at it, they get angry and frustrated. We all want to succeed. We all want our lives to have value, to matter, and to make a difference. So does God. It's in our DNA from the moment we exit our mother's womb.

I've never had anyone say to me in all my years of walking this planet, "You know, Jimmy, I believe God birthed me on this planet to fail."

Then the third evidence is God provides us with the resources to get there. We all have built-in interests, passions, ideas, talents, abilities, strengths, spiritual gifts, opportunities, education, and relationships that God has invested in our lives in order for us to pursue success as He has defined it.

In Luke 22:24-27, the disciples were moving toward the final days with Jesus and His life on earth. These disciples had been with Him from the beginning, were His closest followers, and supposedly understood His teaching, but they were arguing about who was going to be the greatest among them when Jesus finally comes into His kingdom. They wanted to know who was going to be the most successful.

> *A dispute also arose among them, as to which of them was to be regarded as the greatest. And Jesus said to them, "The kings of the Gentiles exercise lordship over them, and those in authority over them are called benefactors. But not so with you. Rather, let the greatest among you become as the youngest, and the leader as one who serves. For who is the greater, one who reclines at table or one who serves? Is it not the one who reclines at table? But I am among you as the one who serves."*

Notice Jesus did not reprimand them for the ambition to be great or to be successful. He didn't address that issue at all because it's what He wants for His followers. What Jesus addressed was how they were to get there. Jesus wanted them to be a success, but He wanted them to be careful how they defined success. In many ways, the definition of success depends on who you're asking. If I ask a coach, the players, or the fans during bowl season, they'd say, "Winning." If I were to ask a sales person, the answer would be, "Being number one. Leading the company in sales." If I were to ask a parent, the response would be, "It's having godly children." If you work in the marketplace, your answer would be, "Make a living to support myself and my family." A student would say, "Passing the next test, passing the class, and graduating."

We either define success as the world defines it or as God defines it. Our definition and measurement of success will be what determines who we are, what we do, why we do what we do, and what we become.

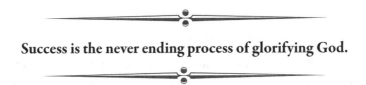

The world defines success as wealth, power, prestige, possessions, achievement, awards, and recognition. We need to know what God's value system is and how it is different from the world's definition in order to define it His way.

Success is the never ending process of glorifying God.

Glorifying God is why God leaves us here after we come into a relationship with Him. We are to bring Him honor and glory, lift up His Name, and make Him look good wherever we are, to whomever we're with, and with whatever we're doing. Success is how we do that because glorifying God is done by becoming who God created us to be. It's fulfilling what He purposed for us to do. It's about discovering His will and His plan for our life and being obedient to it. Living the life He has called us to live reflects the character of God and that is the biblically successful life.

However, there are a lot of people, even Christians that are on the world's page instead of God's. Let me tell you about six men whom the world would have defined as successful.

One: This gentleman was the president of the largest independent steel company at the time. He lived on borrowed money the last five years of his life and he died destitute. His name was Charles Schwab.

155

Two: This gentleman was the president of the New York Stock Exchange. He spent the last years of his life in prison. His name was Richard Whitney.

Three: This man was a member of the President's Cabinet and received a Presidential Pardon at the end of his life in order to go home and die. His name was Albert Fall.

Four: At one time this man was the greatest bear on Wall Street, but he ended up committing suicide. His name was Jesse Livermore.

Five: This man also committed suicide though he was head of the world's largest monopoly at the time. His name was Ivan Krueger.

Six: The one-time president of the Bank of International Settlements, Leon Fraser, also committed suicide.

At one time, you could take the annual income of those six men and it was larger than what was in the United States Treasury. Were they successful? It depends on your definition and measurement of success doesn't it?

How Does God Measure Success?

So, we're climbing the ladder of success, but are we leaning it against the right wall? Go back to Joshua 1:8. God said to Joshua, "This book of the law shall not depart from your mouth, but you shall meditate on it day and night so that you may be careful to do all that is written in it. For then, you will make your way prosperous and then you will have **good success**."

I like the idea that God's word to Joshua has a descriptive term for success. He calls it **good success**. The inference is God's success is good success and any other kind of success is bad success. A good success is a biblically successful life that is described in these first nine verses in

Joshua 1 and are expanded in Deuteronomy 31:7-8 and 23 to give us the full picture.

The first measurement is **dependence**. Success begins with a dependent relationship on God as we read in Deuteronomy 31:7, Joshua 1:5, and 1:9. God is saying if we want to experience success His way, it begins with understanding that we can't do this without Him. We can be independent, self-reliant, and do it our way, and we may experience some measure of success as the world defines it, but it will not be as God has defined it. It will not be good success. The only way to experience God's way of success is by depending and relying on Him.

Joshua could not pull off leading three million Jewish people into the Promised Land without God's help. Jesus said in John 15:5, "Apart from Me you can do nothing." The foundation of a biblically successful life is a life of trust, humility, being teachable, and having an absolute dependency on God. The picture of a small hand in that big hand saying, "I need you, I trust you, I rely on you, I depend on you, indicates  that we acknowledge that apart from God I can't get it done." That small hand is not that of a baby, it's ours and the big hand is God's.

The second measurement is **obedience**. Joshua 1:7-8 says, "Be strong and very courageous, be careful to do according to all the law that Moses my servant commanded you. Do not turn from it to the right or to the left that you may have good success wherever you go. Be careful to do all. This book of the law shall not depart from your mouth, but you shall meditate on it day and night so that you may be careful to do according to all that is written in it."

God measures success by our obedience. There's no way around it and there's no such thing as partial obedience. If obedience is based on our knowledge of Scripture, we must know what it says which requires reading it. Here are the three "R's" of successful obedience:

- Read it (the Bible)
- Reflect on it
- Reproduce it

I know some people who have proudly confessed they read through the Bible every year, but there is little or no evidence of its principles reflected in their everyday lives. We need to read it and reflect on it. We need to think about and ask questions about what we're reading. Then we need to pray and ask God to help us to implement what we have read in our life through obedience. Most of what you and I need to know about what God wants us to do is right in the Bible either by way of clear command or by way of principle.

Third is the measurement of **service**. Joshua 1:1 says, "After the death of Moses, the servant of the Lord, the Lord said to Joshua, the son of Nun, Moses' assistant, Moses my servant." Twice God refers to Moses as His servant. God is saying I have had a servant for all of these years, now I'm handing that mantle of serving and leading My people into the Promised Land over to you, Joshua. I am placing that servant leadership responsibility on you.

"You shall cause this people to inherit the land that I swore to their fathers." As a result of serving and taking the talents, abilities, resources, opportunity, and training invested in Joshua, God is going to use him to lead His people to experience a new land, a land of promise. If we're going to be biblically successful, we've got to serve and invest in others.

We can't just sit there. We need to actively do something with all that we have been given.

If success is defined according to the worldly measurement, Jesus was an utter failure and yet we follow Him. None of us believe we're following an utter failure.

Jesus lived a supremely successful life as God defines and measures it. He lived a life of total dependence, complete obedience, and absolute service to God.

Success God's Way

Number One: Success God's way is a process. It's a journey. It's not a destination, it's not an arrival. We'll spend the rest of our lives chasing, pursuing, and climbing the ladder of success. We've just got to make sure it's leaning against the right wall.

Number Two: Success God's way will not always be easy. That's why twice in Deuteronomy and three times in the Joshua passage, God told Joshua to be strong and courageous. It's got its bumps in the road, it's got its curves, it's got its bends, and it's going to be difficult at times to stand up and be who we need to be and to do what we need to do in order to be biblically successful. It's that inner strength God infuses in each of us through our dependence on Him that produces the courage and the staying, enduring, persevering power when things get tough. We have to push our way through with God's help.

Number Three: It's never too late to find success His way. Success His way is for everybody. It's not about the economy. It's not about wealth. It isn't about status. It's not about recognition. It's not about achievements. It's about dependence, obedience, and service to God which means every one of us can live a biblically successful life. It's a choice we each have to make. It begins by answering the questions posed at the beginning of this chapter.

- *So is it permissible for a Christian to pursue success?*
- *Can a Christian live a godly life and pursue success simultaneously?*
- *Is God even interested in our being a success?*
- *How do we achieve godly success?*

The Documentary of Your Life

Imagine there has been a film crew documenting your life. They have traveled with you for the last five years. Wherever you went, whoever you were with, whatever you did, and whatever you said has been documented. Now they have put an hour and a half documentary together about you and invited people to go and watch it.

When these people exit the documentary of the last five years of your life, how do you think they would define and measure your success? What would they say? Are you okay with what they would say? More importantly, is God okay with it? What changes do you need to make to become more dependent, more obedient, and more of a servant to God now that you know what wall to lean your ladder of success against?

QUESTIONS FOR SELF REFLECTION
CHAPTER THIRTEEN—SUCCESS GOD'S WAY

1. *Every facet of our lives is impacted by how we view success, yet it's something we rarely talk about.*

    How do you view success?

    How do you define it?

    How do you think it ought to be measured?

2. *How does the world define success?*

3. *How does God's value system differ from the world's value system?*

4. *How does God measure success?*

5. *What changes do you need to make to become more dependent, more obedient, and more of a servant to God now that you know what wall to lean your ladder of success against? I asked this question at the end of the chapter. Now write out an answer...*

6. *What was your best learning from this chapter?*

Final Word

Keep Growing as a Leader

Mark Twain made these comments concerning a friend of his who had passed away, "He died at thirty, we buried him at sixty. He quit growing. He quit learning."

One of the quotes that I gave you at the beginning of the book was from Andy Stanley. "The more you know about leadership, the faster you grow as a leader and the farther you go as a leader."[2]

We have talked about how important our commitment and dedication as well as our effectiveness at getting the job done is to our impact and our influence as a leader. In the end, the measurement of our lives is determined by how many other lives we touched and influenced. So, we've got to keep building and growing this leadership quotient.

Our core Scripture, Psalm 78:72 says, "David shepherded them with integrity of heart, and with skillful hands he led them." We need to do whatever we can to improve our character and make it more like Christ. Competency is identifying the few things at which we are exceptional, and then learn more about them, and intentionally practice them as a way of

---

[2] "Next Generation Leader" by Andy Stanley, p 9.

life. We aren't to be ordinary. We are to be extraordinary. We are to build relationships and care about others.

Anything we try to improve in these areas will help us to continue to grow and develop as leaders.

Number One: Be a Continual Learner. Never feel you have learned all there is to know. Growth means you are always moving forward. Once you stagnate, you begin to die.

Number Two: Be a Reader. Read books, articles, and anything else you can get your hands on to stay current with today's world. Twenty-seven percent of the American population never reads a book. The average American reads five books a year at the most. If you read for 15 minutes a day, you'll read fifteen books in a year.

Number Three: Serve. Leaders are servants. Look for a chance to make an impact at home, at work, in the community, and at church. Leadership is about service, not about sitting around.

Number Four: Watch and Listen. Leaders are watchers and listeners. Two or three times a year, write out and take 10-12 questions you would like answered and approach somebody that might be able to answer them for you. Interview them and learn from them. Watch people. Learn from them. Draw knowledge and wisdom from them.

Number Five: Connect with Other Leaders. Look for opportunities to connect with other people who are hungry to grow and to develop. That's going to feed you and it's going to help you to develop as well.

Number Six: Access Quality Training. It's never been more accessible to continue to grow and to develop as a leader. Quality training is out there if you look for it.

Number Seven: Invest in Developing Other Leaders. Nothing will grow you more and faster than investing in someone else. Get somebody younger than you are and help develop them, invest in them, and add value into their lives. Read a book together and get together at 7 o'clock in the morning at Starbucks for an hour to talk about it. It's not that hard. Just do it.

Number Eight: Stay Accountable. Don't float out there by yourself. Keep that character in check. Find a coach. Find a mentor. Find a friend. Find a peer.

Number Nine: Think Often of Your Legacy. How do you want to be remembered? The best advice I can give you is to live that way. Tim McGraw has a song that says, "Live Like You Were Dying."

Number Ten: Seek Opportunities for Expanded Influence. Constantly be on the lookout for any opportunity to make a difference and add value in the lives of people.

Everyone is in the leadership business. Anytime we attempt to influence the thinking, attitudes, or behaviors of another person we have assumed a leadership role (which we all do many times every day). You (and I) do lead to some degree. The only question is, "How effective are we?" Greater impact and influence results when you truly grasp *"It's All about Leadership"* by striving to *be a Leader Worth Following*.

As we come to an end of our study on leadership, I have a final question for self-reflection for you. Each chapter, I have been asking you to examine your leadership, explore ways to grow, learn, and mature as God's leader in the world, in your community, in the workplace, in the church, in the family, and in all your relationships. Every follower of Christ is a leader. Remember, someone is watching you, learning from you, and following words and actions of yours. So here's my question:

Is Your Leadership Effective in Leading Others to Christ?

In other words, do people see, hear, and experience the living presence of Jesus Christ through your leadership? Are you willing to continue to grow and learn as a leader? I am praying that what I have shared with you in this book will not only encourage, equip, and empower you as a leader, but that you will share all that you have learned in raising up other leaders for Christ and His Kingdom.

"Greatest Leadership Learnings"

1. Leadership is not about you.
2. All leadership is interim and temporary. No one leads forever.
3. The best leadership is character-driven.
4. Great leaders first lead themselves well.
5. Value is measured by your generosity.
6. I am human and can only do so much. I cannot do it all (and I don't need to).
7. The purpose of leading is serving. Lead for the right reason.
8. Choose effectiveness over being right.
9. When the leader gets better, everybody wins. (Bill Hybels)
10. Leadership is not about having all the answers.
11. Great leaders are great followers first.
12. Choose relationships over rules.
13. Don't make leadership too important.
14. One of the most important things you can do as a leader is to invest in and create more leaders.
15. Ask more questions, not give more answers.
16. It takes great courage to lead well.
17. Our capacity to grow determines our capacity to lead.
18. Leadership is more about who you are than what you do.

19. Leadership is no place to hide.
20. The real joy of leadership is found in the journey not the destination.

Background Reading and Resources for Chapters

Chapter 1

Jeffrey Cohn and Jay Moran, *Why Are We Bad at Picking Good Leaders: A Better Way to Evaluate Leadership Potential* (San Francisco: Jossey-Bass, 2011), 4 (See also 243).

John C. Maxwell, *The 21 Irrefutable Laws of Leadership: Follow Them and People Will Follow You*, rev. ed. (Nashville, TN: Thomas Nelson, 2007), 1-9.

Ken Blanchard, "Leadership as an Influence Process," *howwe-lead.org* (blog), March 1, 2010, http://howwelead.org/2010/03/01/leadership-as-an-influence-process/.

Thom Rainer, "The Main Reason People Leave a Church," *Thom S. Rainer* (blog), January 21, 2013 http://thomrainer.com/2013/01/the-main-reason-people-leave-a-church/.

"Christians: More Like Jesus or Pharisees?" www.barna.org, April 30, 2013, https://www.barna.org/barna-update/faith-spirituality/611-christians-more-like-jesus-orpharisees#.Vd3k4GpRFyc.

Henry T. Blackaby and Richard Blackaby, *Spiritual Leadership: Moving People On to God's Agenda* (Nashville, TN: Broadman & Holman Publishers, 2001), xi.

Chapter 2

Tom Rath and Barry Conchie, *Strengths Based Leadership: Great Leaders, Teams, and Why People Follow* (New York: Gallup Press, 2008), 80-91.

Henry T. Blackaby and Richard Blackaby, *Spiritual Leadership: Moving People On to God's Agenda* (Nashville, TN: Broadman & Holman Publishers, 2001), 13-14.

Chapter 3

Andy Stanley, *Louder Than Words* (Sisters, OR: Multnomah Publishers, 2004), 19.

Chapter 4

Geoffrey Colvin, *Talent Is Overrated: What Really Separates World-Class Performers from Everybody Else*, pbk. ed. (New York: Portfolio, 2010), 1.

John C. Maxwell, Stephen R. Graves, and Thomas G. Addington, *Life@work: Marketplace Success for People of Faith* (Nashville, TN: Thomas Nelson Publishers, 2005), 39-40.

The Gallup organization has developed an assessment called StrengthsFinder that is an excellent tool for discovering your greatest talents. I cannot recommend this resource strongly enough. For more information, go to https://www.gallupstrengthscenter.com/

Tom Rath, *Strengths Finder 2.0* (New York: Gallup Press, 2007), i-iv.

Chapter 5

Marshall Goldsmith and Mark Reiter, *What Got You Here Won't Get You There: How Successful People Become Even More Successful* (New York, NY: Hyperion, 2007), 40-41.

Tim Elmore, "Why Is It Hard to Find Good Male Leaders On Campus? *Growing Leaders* (blog), n.d., http://growingleaders.com/blog/male-leaders/.

Charles R. Swindoll, *Dropping Your Guard: The Value of Open Relationships* (Waco, TX: Word Books, 1983), 122-23.

C. S. Lewis, *The Four Loves* (London: William Collins Sons and Co., 1960), 169.

Chapter 7

Dee Hock, source unknown.

Bill George et al., "Discovering Your Authentic Leadership," *Harvard Business Review* (February 2007).

Chapter 8

Brian Dodd, "The One Thing Every Leader Must Do," *Brian Dodd on Leadership* (blog), May 14, 2011, http://www.briandoddonleadership.com/2011/05/14/the-one-thing-every-leader-must-do/.

Chapter 9

Susan Sorenson and Keri Garman, "How to Tackle U.S. Employees' Stagnating Engagement," Gallup.com, June 11, 2013, http://www.gallup.com/businessjournal/162953/tackle-employeesstagnating-engagement.aspx.

Chapter 10

Stephen M R. Covey and Rebecca R. Merrill, *The Speed of Trust: The One Thing That Changes Everything* (New York: Free Press, 2008, 2006).

RECOMMENDED READING

Anderson, Leith. *Leadership That Works*. Minneapolis: Bethany House, 1999.

Anderson, Robert C. *The Effective Pastor*. Chicago: Moody Press, 1985.

Barna, George. *Leaders on Leadership*. Ventura, CA: Regal, 1997.

_____. *A Fish Out of Water*. Nashville: Integrity Publishers, 2002.

Blackaby, Henry. *Spiritual Leadership*. Nashville: Broadman and Holman, 2001.

Biehl, Bob. *Increasing Your Leadership Confidence*. Sisters, OR: Questar Publishers, 1989.

Blanchard, Ken and Hodges, Phil. *The Servant Leader: Transforming Your Heart, Head, Hands, and Habits*. Nashville: Countryman, 2003.

_____. *Lead Like Jesus*. Nashville: W Publishing Group, 2005.

_____ and Miller, Mark. *The Secret: What Great Leaders Know and Do*. San Francisco: BerrettKoehler Publishers, 2007.

Boa, Kenneth. *The Perfect Leader: Practicing the Leadership Traits of God*. Colorado Springs, CO: Cook Communications, 2006.

Bonem, Mike and Patterson, Roger. *Leading from the Second Chair*. San Francisco: Jossey-Bass, 2005.

Borek, John, Lovett, Danny and Towns, Elmer. *The Good Book on Leadership: Case Studies from the Bible.* Nashville: Broadman & Holman Publishers, 2005.

Bryant, Andrew and Kazan, Ana. *Self Leadership.* New York: The McGraw-Hill Companies, 2013.

Buckingham, Marcus and Coffman, Curt. *First, Break All the Rules: What the World's Greatest Managers Do Differently.* New York: Simon and Schuster, 1999.

_____. *GO Put Your Strengths to Work: 6 Powerful Steps to Achieve Outstanding Performance.* New York: Free Press, 2007.

_____ and Clifton, Donald O. *Now, Discover Your Strengths.* New York: The Free Press, 2001.

_____. *The One Thing You Need to Know… About Great Managing, Great Leading, and Sustained Individual Success.* New York: Free Press, 2005.

Charan, Ram. *Know-How: The 8 Skills that Separate People Who Perform from Those Who Don't.* New York: Crown Publishing Group, 2007.

Christensen, Clayton, M. *How Will You Measure Your Life?* New York: HarperCollins Publishers, 2012.

Clinton, J. Robert. *The Making of a Leader.* Colorado Springs: NavPress, 1988.

Cloud, Henry. *Integrity: The Courage to Meet the Demands of Reality.* New York: Harper Collins Publishers, 2006.

_____ *Necessary Endings.* New York: HarperCollins Publishers, 2010.

Cohn, Jeffrey and Moran, Jay. *Why Are We Bad at Picking Good Leaders?* San Francisco, CA: Jossey-Bass, 2011.

Collins, Jim. *Good to Great.* New York: Harper Collins Publishers, Inc., 2001.

Cordeiro, Wayne. *The Dream Releasers.* Ventura, CA: Regal, 2002.

2

_____. *Leading on Empty*. Bloomington, MN: Bethany House Publishers, 2009.

_____. *Sifted*. Grand Rapids, MI: Zondervan, 2012.

Crosby, Harriet. *Devotions for Leaders*. San Francisco: Jossey-Bass, 2002.

Eims, Leroy. *Be the Leader You Were Meant to Be*. Wheaton: Victor Books, 1977.

Engstrom, Ted W. *The Making of a Christian Leader*. Grand Rapids: Zondervan, 1976.

Faulkner, Brooks R. *Getting On Top of Your Work*. Nashville: Convention Press, 1999.

Ferguson, Chuck and Duin, Steve. *Indomitable Spirit: Life-Changing Lessons in Leadership*. Portland, OR: Agora Publishing, 2004.

Fisher, David. *The 21ˢᵗ Century Pastor*. Grand Rapids: Zondervan, 1996.

Fisher, Roger and Sharp, Alan. *Getting It Done*. New York: Harper Collins Publishers, 1998.

Ford, Leighton. *Transforming Leadership*. Downers Grove, Ill: InterVarsity Press, 1999.

Forman, Rawland, Jones, Jeff and Miller, Bruce. *The Leadership Baton*. Grand Rapids: Zondervan, 2004.

Gangel, Kenneth O. *Team Leadership in Christian Ministry*. Chicago: Moody Press, 1997.

_____. *Feeding and Leading*. Wheaton: Victor Books, 1989.

George, Bill. *True North*. San Francisco, CA: Jossey-Bass Publishers, 2007.

Goffee, Rob and Jones, Gareth. *Why Should Anyone Be Led by You?* Boston: Harvard Business School Press, 2006.

Goldsmith, Marshall. *What Got You Here Won't Get You There*. New York: Hyperion Books, 2007.

Graves, Stephen R. and Addington, Thomas G. *Life@Work on Leadership*. San Francisco: Jossey-Bass, 2002.

Guinness, Os. *The Call: Finding and Fulfilling the Central Purpose of Your Life*. Nashville: Word Publishing, 1998.

Hamm, John. *Unusually Excellent*. San Francisco, CA: Jossey-Bass, 2011.

Harper, Tom. *Leading from the Lions' Den*. Nashville: B&H Publishing Group, 2010.

Hughes, Kent. *Liberating Ministry from the Success Syndrome*. Wheaton: Tyndale House Publishers, 1987.

Hybels, Bill. *Courageous Leadership*. Grand Rapids: Zondervan Publishing House, 2002.

_____. *Axiom: Powerful Leadership Proverbs*. Grand Rapids: Zondervan Publishing House, 2008.

Ingram, Chip. *Good to Great in God's Eyes: Ten Practices Great Christians Have in Common*. Grand Rapids: Baker Books, 2007.

Iorg, Jeff. *The Character of Leadership*. Nashville: B & H Publishing Group, 2007.

Irwin, Tim. *Run with the Bulls without Getting Trampled*. Nashville: Thomas Nelson, 2006.

_____. *Derailed*. Nashville: Thomas Nelson, 2009.

Jarvis, Mike and Peck, Jonathan. *Skills for Life*. Boston: Skills for Life LLC, 2003.

Klann, Gene. *Building Character*. San Francisco, CA: Jossey-Bass, 2007.

Kouzes, James and Posner, Barry. *The Truth About Leadership*. San Francisco, CA: Jossey-Bass, 2010.

_____. *Credibility: How Leaders Gain and Lose It—Why People Demand It*. San Francisco, CA: Jossey-Bass, 2011.

Kramp, John. *On Track Leadership*. Nashville: B & H Publishing Group, 2006.

Krzyzewski, Mike. *Leading with the Heart*. New York: Warner Books, 2000.

Kubicek, Jeremie. *Leadership Is Dead*. New York: Howard Books, 2011.

Lomenick, Brad. *The Catalyst Leader.* Nashville: Thomas Nelson, 2013.

Loritts, Crawford W., Jr. *Leadership as an Identity.* Chicago, IL: Moody Publishers, 2009.

Malphurs, Aubrey. *Being Leaders.* Grand Rapids: Baker Books, 2003.

_____. *Building Leaders.* Grand Rapids: Baker Books, 2004.

Marshall, Tom. *Understanding Leadership.* Grand Rapids: Baker Books, 2003.

Maxwell, John. *Developing the Leader Within You.* Nashville: Thomas Nelson, 1993.

_____. *Developing the Leaders Around You.* Nashville: Thomas Nelson, 1995.

_____. *Life@Work: Marketplace Success for People of Faith.* Nashville: Thomas Nelson, 2005.

_____. *Talent Is Never Enough.* Nashville: Thomas Nelson, 2007.

_____. *Winning with People.* Nashville: Thomas Nelson, 2004.

McNeal, Reggie. *A Work of Heart: Understanding How God Shapes Spiritual Leaders.* San Francisco: Jossey-Bass Publishers, 2000.

_____. *Practicing Greatness: 7 Disciplines of Extraordinary Spiritual Leaders.* San Francisco: Jossey-Bass, 2006.

Miller, Calvin. *The Empowered Leader: 10 Keys to Servant Leadership.* Nashville: Broadman & Holman Publishers, 1995.

Morris, Gregory. *In Pursuit of Leadership.* Xulon Press, 2006.

Mullins, Tom. *The Leadership Game.* Nashville: Thomas Nelson, 2005.

Pink, Daniel. *Drive.* New York: Riverhead Books, 2009.

Phillips, Donald T. *Lincoln on Leadership: Executive Strategies for Tough Times.* New York: Warner Books, 2002.

Rath, Tom. *StrengthsFinder 2.0.* New York: Gallup Press, 2007.

_____. and Conchie, Barry. *Strengths Based Leadership.* New York: Gallup Press, 2008.

Reccord, Bob and Singer, Randy. *Made to Count: Discovering What to Do with Your Life*. Nashville: Word Publishing Group, 2004.

Reynolds, Siimon. *Why People Fail*. San Francisco, CA: Josey-Bass, 2012

Rima, Samuel D. *Leading from the Inside Out*. Grand Rapids: Baker Books, 2000.

Rinehart, Stacy T. *Upside Down: The Paradox of Servant Leadership*. Colorado Springs, CO: NavPress, 1998.

Saccone, Steve. *Relational Intelligence*. San Francisco: Jossey-Bass, 2009.

Sample, Steven. *The Contrarian's Guide to Leadership*. San Francisco: Jossey-Bass, 2002.

Sanborn, Mark. *You Don't Need a Title to Be a Leader*. New York: Doubleday, 2006.

Sanders, J. Oswald. *Spiritual Leadership*. Chicago: Moody Press, 1994.

Smith, Dean. *The Carolina Way: Leadership Lessons from a Life in Coaching*. New York: The Penguin Press, 2004.

Stanley, Andy. *The Next Generation Leader*. Sisters, OR: Multnomah Publishers, 2003.

_____. *Visioneering: God's Blueprint for Developing and Maintaining Vision*. Sisters, OR: Multnomah, 1999.

Stark, David. *Christ-Based Leadership*. Minneapolis: Bethany House, 2005.

Sumner, Sarah. *Leadership Above the Line*. Carol Stream, IL: Tyndale, 2006.

Thomas, Curtis C. *Practical Wisdom for Pastors: Words of Encouragement for a Lifetime of Ministry*. Wheaton: Crossway Books, 2001.

White, John. *Excellence in Leadership*. Downers Grove, Ill: InterVarsity Press, 1986.

Williams, Pat. *The Paradox of Power: A Transforming View of Leadership*. Warner Books, 2002.

_____. *Leadership Excellence*. Uhrichsville, OH: Barbour Publishing, Inc., 2012.

Winseman, Albert L., Clifton, Donald O. and Liesveld, Curt. *Living Your Strengths*. New York: Gallup Press, 2003.

Wooden, John and Jamison, Steve. *Wooden on Leadership*. New York: McGraw-Hill, 2005.

Zigarmi, Drea, O'Connor, Michael, Blanchard, Ken and Edeburn, Carl. *The Leader Within*. Upper Saddle River, New Jersey: Pearson Education, Inc, 2005.

BIOGRAPHICAL SKETCH

Jimmy Knott
Teaching Pastor

Jimmy Knott serves as Teaching Pastor and oversees leader development at First Baptist Orlando in Orlando, Florida. He is a native of Tennessee and received his high school diploma from Peabody High in 1968. He earned his B.S. degree in Chemical Engineering at the University of Tennessee in 1973. That same year, he married Linda Lewis.

After working as an engineer for the DuPont Company in Nashville, Jimmy felt the Lord's leadership into full-time ministry. He enrolled at New Orleans Theological Seminary, and earned his M. Div. in 1976. While attending seminary, Jimmy served as Associate Pastor of Lakeside Baptist Church in Metarie, Louisiana.

Following graduation from New Orleans Baptist Theological Seminary, Jimmy and Linda moved to Nashville, Tennessee, where Jimmy assumed the position of Minister of Youth, College & Career at Two

Rivers Baptist Church. He was ordained to the Gospel Ministry at Two Rivers in May 1975. Jimmy has been on staff at First Baptist Orlando since June 1980, and currently serves as the Teaching Pastor and oversees Leadership Development. Jimmy earned his Doctor of Ministry degree from New Orleans Baptist Theological Seminary in May 2002.

Jimmy has also authored numerous books and has served as a leadership coach for more than ten years. He is much in demand as a Bible teacher, preacher, and conference leader.

He and Linda, a housewife who holds a B.S. in Pharmacy, have four adult children: Stephanie, Jeremy, Jonathan, and Justin, and three grandchildren: Tyler, Alyssa, and James. Hobbies of Jimmy's center around family and sports-related activities. He enjoys golf, reading, and coaching basketball.

To learn more about Leadership and Ministry resources go to jandlministry.com/leadership.

Appendix 1:

What Are My Core Values?

Below are some examples of core values that affect how we serve and influence others. Look at the list, add others as needed, and try to decide your top four.

Core Values			
Balance	Courage	Dignity	Duty
Effectiveness	Equality	Excellence	Faith
Faithfulness	Flexibility	Freedom	Humor
Integrity	Honesty	Honor	Hope
Humility	Inner Peace	Joy	Justice
Kindness	Love	Loyalty	Perseverance
Positive Attitude	Relationships	Respect	Safety
Service	Trust	Truth	Wholeness

My top four core values are:

1. _____ 3. _____

2. _____ 4. _____

─────────────── QUESTION ───────────────

Why don't you ask some people close to you to identify what
they think is really important to you based on how they see you live?

─────────────── for REFLECTION ───────────────

When we are not clear about our values or when our actions contradict our stated beliefs, we short-change ourselves in the areas of our own credibility, performance, and confidence. We set up an inner conflict within ourselves.

Appendix 2:

Where Is My Character Flawed?

CHARACTER QUESTIONS	Rarely	Sometimes	Usually	Almost
1. I take personal responsibility for my actions.	1	2	3	4
2. I treat all people the same.	1	2	3	4
3. When I make a promise I fulfill it.	1	2	3	4
4. I will do the right thing even when it is difficult.	1	2	3	4
5. I make decisions for the good of others when another choice would benefit me.	1	2	3	4
6. I am quick to recognize others for their efforts and contributions to my success.	1	2	3	4

	1	2	3	4
7. My decisions are based on biblical standards and convictions.	1	2	3	4
8. What I expect from others is consistent with what I expect of myself.	1	2	3	4
9. I maintain self-control.	1	2	3	4
10. I am totally honest with people.	1	2	3	4
11. I am the same person, no matter who I am with or the circumstances.	1	2	3	4
12. Is the "visible" me and the "real" me consistent?	1	2	3	4
Total =				

Appendix 3:

Paul's Journey

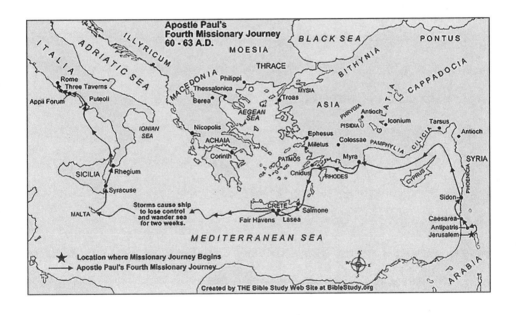